COME,
SEE A MAN

Lillian Gold

WestBow
PRESS
A DIVISION OF THOMAS NELSON

WestBow Press books may be ordered through booksellers or by contacting:

WestBow Press
A Division of Thomas Nelson
1663 Liberty Drive
Bloomington, IN 47403
www.westbowpress.com
1-(866) 928-1240

ISBN: 978-1-4497-8277-1 (sc)

Library of Congress Control Number: 2013901273

Printed in the United States of America

WestBow Press rev. date: 1/28/2013

Table of Contents

This book is dedicated to

My true love, Deacon Quincy Gold
My deceased parents
All my children and family

Special Thanks to

The Powerhouse Church of Jesus Christ
Delorise McDuffie

Preface

The title of this book, *Come, see a Man*, is taken from the Gospel of John 4th chapter, 4th through the 29th verses. In this chapter, the apostle John tells the story about the unnamed woman Jesus met at the well. She was a Samaritan, a people who had intermarried and were considered to be unclean and despised by the Jews. And because of her immoral sexual behavior, she was also considered to be a sinful woman. Perhaps for this reason she came out to draw water in the midday heat to avoid the gossip of the women who came to draw water at the end of the day. As the woman came to the well, she saw a man sitting there. She was really caught by surprise when the man, being a Jew, said to her, "Will you give me a drink." Thus the woman said to him, "You are a Jew and I am a Samaritan woman. How can you ask me for a drink?" Seeing how this woman came out to draw water in the heat of the day, Jesus recognized her desperation for something to satisfy her thirsty soul. Therefore he tried to help her understand her need by telling her about the living water. Jesus said, "Everyone who drinks this water will be thirsty again, but whoever drinks the water I give him will never thirst. Indeed the water I give him will become in him a spring of water welling up to eternal life." Not understanding what Jesus was saying, the woman said to Him, "Sir, give me this water so that I won't get thirsty and have to keep coming here to draw water." William Barclay, a world-renowned New Testament interpreter said, "At the heart of this there is the fundamental truth that in the human heart there is a thirst for something that only Jesus Christ can satisfy...In every man [and woman] there is this nameless unsatisfied longing; this vague discontent; this lacking something, this frustration."[1]

Still not understanding what Jesus was trying to tell her, He said to the woman, "Go, call your husband and come back." Shocked by his knowledge of her, she felt compelled to face the truth about herself, and so she confessed "I have no husband." Then Jesus said to her, "You are right when you say you have no husband. The fact is, you have had five husbands, and the man you now live with is not your husband. What you have just said is quite true." Indeed, the woman

1   The Daily Study Bible Series, The Gospel of John Volume 1, Revised Edition, Westminster John Knox Press, Louisville, Kentucky 1975, page 155

had five failed marriages, and she was not married to the man that she was currently living with. She was truly amazed that this man she had never met before knew so much about her past. He knew all about her heartaches, the pain and sorrows she had suffered and the difficult times she had in her life. He did not condemn her but showed her love and compassion as no one ever done before. This meeting with Jesus changed her life. The story ends with her leaving her water jar and running back to town to tell the people, "Come, see a man who told me everything I ever did. Could this be the Christ?"

Come, see a Man is the story about Mercy, a woman who could identify with the unnamed woman who met Jesus at the well. Like the woman at the well, Mercy also had a thirst deep down in her soul for love. God created us this way. All human beings are born with an innate desire to be loved and accepted. In the beginning, after making the man "The Lord God said, 'It is not good for the man to be alone;'" and so He made the woman to be a suitable mate for the man.[2] Anyone who saw the winner of the Academy Award movie "Casablanca,"[3] and heard Dooley Wilson sing "As Time Goes By,"[4] will agree that this is true: "Woman needs man and man must have a mate that no one can deny."

As Mercy grew up in a household that was void of

---

2   Genesis 2:18

3   Julius and Philip Epstein and Howard Koch, 1942

4   Written by Herman Hupfeld

any expressions of affection, she craved these feelings and in her early teens she started out on a mission to find love, not knowing what she was looking for. Thus, while on this mission, Mercy suffered a lot of heartaches and emotional pain. At the age of sixteen, she married an older man for all the wrong reasons. In an interview for the December (2009) issue of *Glamour Magazine*, First Lady Michelle Obama said, "Cute's good. But cute only lasts for so long, and it's, 'Who are you as a person?' Don't look at the bankbook or the title. Look at the heart. Look at the soul. When you're dating a man, you should always feel good... You shouldn't be in a relationship with somebody who doesn't make you completely happy and make you whole." Unfortunately, Mercy had to learn this the hard way.

Like Mercy and the unnamed woman at the well, so many women and men in their search for love find themselves in wrong relationships and failed marriages. Mercy had two unsuccessful marriages to abusive men that almost destroyed her. And when she could not find the love she was looking for, she tried to fill this void by turning to alcohol, material possessions and other things, and still she found no satisfaction. Sadly, life for Mercy became unbearably painful, and she felt like giving up before she realized the love she was searching for was with her all the time. It was not until she accepted Christ in her life and had given up on her search to find love outside of herself, did she discover the love of God within her and was able to give as well as receive love. Only then was she ready to meet the right man and have a successful marriage. Perhaps some of the readers of this book will see themselves in Mercy's story and come to the awareness of the need to have Christ in their life to show them the way to true love. *Come, see a Man* was written for the readers to know that Jesus Christ the Son of God is The Man!

Lillian Gold

Prologue

Mercy was born on a forty acre farm in the segregated south. The farm was owned by her maternal grandfather, Noah Jones, who inherited the forty acres and a mule from his ancestors who survived the cruelty of slavery. He was a single parent raising five children whose mother died while they were still young. While caring for the children he also cared for cows, pigs, horses, mules and other farm animals. The fertile soil on the land enabled him to grow and sell tobacco for a profit that enabled him to provide for the needs of his family. The corn, fruits and vegetables that he grew were plentiful for the family to eat. When he was not taking care of his children or farming, he worked as a carpenter and built most of the houses, churches, schools, and stores in the county. Although he received little formal education, he taught himself to count, speak, read and write very well. Needless to say, Mr. Jones was a hard working man who was highly respected by both the White and the Colored people. As a way of relaxation, socializing, and hearing the latest news from around the world and the county, he went to town on Saturday evenings to play checkers with the White folks sitting on the porch of the local general store. He was also a devoted Christian who was trusted with the church treasury. Even with five young children to raise all the unmarried women in town considered Mr. Jones to be a prize catch. However, after the death of his wife he never remarried.

Mr. Jones spent a lot of time out in the fields working on the farm, leaving her mother, Elizabeth, with the responsibility to care for her four younger siblings. She had to make sure all the children, from the youngest age five to the oldest age eleven, did their morning and evening chores. They had to feed the chickens and gather the eggs, feed the pigs and the other farm animals, milk the cow and churn the butter, chop the wood and bring it into the house to start a fire on the stoves, go to the spring to draw water and heat some on the stove so that they could wash up before school. Everyone went to bed at sundown and rose early in the morning before daybreak. Elizabeth had to make breakfast, prepare their lunch boxes, and help the younger children wash up and dress for school; and after school she had to see that they did their homework. Elizabeth missed a lot of days from school to stay home to cook, wash and iron clothes or to care for a sick child. In the summer when school was out, all the children worked out in the fields under the scorching hot sun beside the hired hands pulling tobacco leaves, then curing and preparing the tobacco to sell at the market. Indeed, this was hard labor for the young children and an overwhelming responsibility for a girl thirteen. But Elizabeth and her siblings did what they had to do knowing better not to complain or protest.

Although Mr. Jones was kind hearted, he was a very strict man who did not believe in sparing the switch. Whenever one of his children misbehaved, he would send the child out to the yard to bring back a limb from a bush, and after stripping the limb of all the leaves, he would use it to whip the child across the legs until whelps appeared (No one ever accused him of child abuse). Mr. Jones believed that children should be seen and not heard, well mannered addressing adults as sir or mam. He raised them in the fear of God and taught them that all bad children die and go to the devil. He never showed the children any form of affection believing hugs and kisses spoiled a child. And out of fear of giving the children swelled heads, he never gave them any praises for the things they did well, but he followed the teachings of Proverbs, believing that "Pride goes before destruction[5]."

At the age of nineteen, Elizabeth married a man, Ezekiel Mills, of mixed race who was an abandoned

5   Proverbs 16:18

orphan. Ezekiel did not know his parents or any relatives. From the time he was a small boy, he was raised on a farm by a White family who took him in and brought him up until he was a young man. The family treated him as one of their own, but like Mr. Jones they didn't show him any form of affection. And although he could pass for White, he attended segregated Colored schools and grew up confused not knowing for sure if he was Colored or White. Perhaps Ezekiel felt comfortable around Colored people was the reason he would walk two miles to sit on the porch and talk with Elizabeth and the other members of the family.

One Sunday after church Ezekiel came to visit the family as usual, asked Mr. Jones for Elizabeth's hand, and proposed to her void of any feelings of romantic love. Seeing how Ezekiel was "good looking," light skin with straight hair and a nice man with good manners, Elizabeth accepted his proposal. A few days later she dressed in her Sunday best, and the two traveled by a mule drawn wagon to the Court House to be married by the Justice of Peace. They arrived back home in the evening in time for Elizabeth to cook supper for her family and her new husband. She set the table with the white lace tablecloth used only on holidays and special occasions, and the dishes and glasses used only when the family entertained company. Then everyone sat down at the table, and after Mr. Jones asked the Lord's blessings for the food, they dined on smothered chicken, butter beans, stewed tomatoes, corn pudding, biscuits, cake with brown sugar icing, and lemonade. After supper Mr. Jones brought out a Mason jar of moonshine whiskey to toast the bride and groom. There was no honeymoon. That night the newlyweds slept together on the bed that was reserved for guests, in the front parlor. The next day they were awake at daybreak. Ezekiel went to work on the farm with Mr. Jones, and Elizabeth continued to cook, wash and iron clothes, and take care of her younger siblings as usual.

In spite of what appeared to be a loveless marriage, Elizabeth and Ezekiel had five children. Mercy was their second child, and like the first one, Elizabeth gave birth on the bed in the front parlor and she was brought into the world by a midwife. After Mercy was born, Elizabeth had three more children. While she was still very young, Mercy's parents moved with the family to New York following the migration of the Colored forks leaving the south to seek better jobs up north. Soon after they arrived in New York, Ezekiel passing for White was hired as a waiter at a fancy restaurant down town.

As far back as Mercy could remember her parents never appeared to be happy and they spent very little time together. With their father working so hard for so many hours to pay rent, keep food on the table, cloths on their backs, and keep up with the bills he had little time to spend with the children as well. As a matter of fact the children very seldom saw him since most of the time when he was home he was in the bed sleeping after a hard day at work. Whenever he had time-off and some extra money to spend, he would take the children to the circus, parades, and the movies. Except for the times he had to work, someone was sick, or the weather was too bad to go out, he took the children to church every Sunday. He served on the usher board at Mt. Zion Baptist Church, and all the children attended Sunday school and the children's worship service. And even though Mercy could not sing, she sung on the youth choir. Her father was a quiet man, who didn't have much to say even when he was with the children. Mercy never felt close to her father, he was more like a stranger that she didn't really know.

There was never any display of love or affection in their home—not even between Mercy's parents. She never saw them hold hands, hug or kiss one another as lovers do. And in the same way her parents were raised, they raised their children. When Mercy got older there was no doubt in her mind that her parents loved their children. As an adult she understood that they expressed their love in the way they disciplined and provided for them in the best way they could afford. However, as a child Mercy could not see this. Like her grandfather, her parents were very strict disciplinarians who didn't believe in sparing the rod. She used to hear people say to their children, "I beat you because I love you." When she was growing up she wished that her parents didn't love her so much because the beatings she got sure didn't feel like love. Mercy could not understand why her parents did not hug or kiss her when she was hurt and crying, in the way she saw other parents do with their children. In those times Mercy couldn't help but believe that she was unloved and unwanted. She grew up craving love, and fulfilling this need by reading romantic novels. One of Mercy's favorite books to read was "Gone with the Wind."[6] She was fascinated by the love between Rhett Butler and Scarlett O'Hara. She read this book over and over again until she knew the story by memory and could imagine that she was Scarlett O'Hara, and Rhett Butler was in love with her. While Mercy was still in her early teens, she made up her mind that she was going to find a man to love her, and when she turned eighteen they would get married, live in a big house and have two children.

6   Margaret Mitchell, Macmillian Publishers, 1936

Beloved

All night long on my bed
I looked for the one my heart loves;
I looked for him but did not find him.
I will get up now and go out about the city,
through its streets and squares;
I will search for the one my heart loves.
So I looked for him but did not find him.
The watchmen found me
as they made their rounds in the city.
"Have you seen the one my heart loves?"
Scarcely had I passed them
when I found the one my heart loves.
I held him and would not let him go
till I had brought him to my mother's house,
to the room of the one who conceived me.
Daughters of Jerusalem, I charge you
by the gazelles and by the does of the field:
Do not arouse or awaken love until it so desires.[7]

---

7   Solomon's Song of Songs 3:1-5

CHAPTER 1

The Love of Her Life

Mercy was sixteen and madly in love with Dan Brooks, a twenty-four year old man. He was king of the hill; a real "Dapper Dan," tall, dark and handsome, looking sharp as a tack in tailored made suits, spit shined shoes, diamond ring on his manicured finger, gold watch on his wrist, a clean shaven face and a perfect haircut. He was cool, a real smooth talker, the most popular man in the neighborhood. As Dan held court every evening standing outside the corner bar and grill, young girls as well as older women paraded by saying things like, "He can put his shoes under my bed anytime." And he had the reputation of trying to accommodate as many as he could. His popularity and the way he dressed was one of the reasons Mercy was attracted to him. She also heard that he had velvet lips, and wanted to find out for herself, if that was true.

She was only a kid and knew nothing about love but still she called him the love of her life.

From her early teens, Mercy suffered from low self-esteem and was very insecure, and although some people considered her to be very pretty with long "good" hair, Caucasian facial features and almost as white as her father, she felt ugly. She hated the fact that she was skinny, flat chest and tall for her age. However, no matter how badly Mercy felt about herself, the boys at the high school where she attended didn't see her that way and tried to date her. But she wanted nothing to do with them. She thought that they were too young and too immature for her.

Through a family member Mercy was introduced to James, a young man who was a few years older than her. His family was well off, his father a doctor and his mother a teacher, could afford to send him to New York University. He was the President of his class, good looking, and a perfect Christian gentleman at all times; a man who went to church on Sundays with his parents. James was not a sharp dresser, but he drove a red Cadillac Convertible. Although the car was old and used it was better than having nothing like Dan whose only means of transportation was to walk, take a cab, or ride the subway or the bus. Mercy went out a few times to the movies with James, and he really liked her a lot. Whenever James did not have classes, he would drive down to her school and wait out front for Mercy to come out so that he could drive her home. But she thought that he was square and wanted nothing to do with him either. After school, she would avoid him by going out the back door and take the train home to see Dan standing on the corner. In her young, innocent mind he was gorgeous, fab-u-lous. Whenever she thought about him or whenever she was in his presence, her heart would feel like it was going to jump out of her skin, and beat so loud, like drums beating in her ears. He never seemed to notice her, still she walked pass him as often as she could, praying that one day he would pay her some attention.

Mercy became best friends with a girl named Sarah whose older brother, Philip was friends with Dan. She practically lived in her best friend's house waiting for him to visit. When he did, she would be too nervous to open her mouth to speak to him. And except to politely greet everyone in the room, he had nothing to say to her. While she sat quietly watching his every move, he would go about talking to his friend, paying her little attention. During the summer months, Mercy would go to the beach with Sarah, her brother Philip, and some of his friends, including Dan. There were always women with the men, and they would spend little time in the water and most of the time hiding in the woods somewhere making love. Indeed, it was emotionally painful for Mercy to see Dam with other women in this way. She tried her best to hide her feelings by playing beach volleyball with Sarah and the people they met at the beach. This really was not a good time for her.

That summer Mercy was invited to Sarah's brother, Philip and his girlfriend, Rachel's wedding. They had a grand church wedding with four bridesmaids and groomsmen. Rachel looked like the perfect bride that stepped out of a magazine, in a long white satin dress trimmed in lace and pearls, and a white veil covering her hair and face with a long train that covered the floor of the center isle from the front to the back of the church. This was Mercy's dream wedding; she prayed that one day she would dress up like Rachel and get married in the same way.

Following the wedding, Philip and Rachel held a reception for over two hundred family members and guests at a large catering hall. Dan was there looking as fine as ever. He came alone and sat at the table where she was sitting with Sarah. Champagne flowed like water from a fountain. It was so cool, bubbly, and good that Mercy kept drinking until she was high and had the courage to ask Dan for a dance. He took her into his arms and held her close while they danced to the soft and slow music played by the live band. Feeling overjoyed that she finally had his attention; Mercy laid her head on Dan's shoulders and closed her eyes wishing that the music would never end.

After the wedding reception, Mercy went to Sarah's house where the partying continued. However, she was too drunk to stand up, and passed out in the back room on the bed. While she was knocked out cold, Dan took advantage of her. When Mercy first woke up she thought that she was having a nightmare;

but then she saw that it was no dream. Mercy was too naive at the time to know that she had been raped. All she knew was that Dan had stolen her virginity. It was not suppose to happen this way. Mercy couldn't believe that Dan would do this to her. She was too hurt to talk. And she couldn't tell how he felt or if he believed that he did anything wrong. Dan had nothing to say, he just sat on the edge of the bed with his head held down, and his eyes staring at the floor as if he was too afraid to look her in the face. Mercy just wanted to leave Sarah's house as fast as she could without anyone noticing her. So she pulled herself together, and ran out the house down the street to her home where she went straight into the bathroom to clean herself up. That night she went to bed thanking God that everyone in her household was sleep, and she did not have to answer any questions raised by her mother.

The next time Mercy saw Dan it was a week later at her best friend, Sarah's house. They spoke and never said a word about what had happened. Sarah's brother, Philip was there with Rachel. They had just returned from their honeymoon and were talking about how much they enjoyed their trip to Niagara Falls. This time Mercy did not sit quietly in a corner of the room like she used to, but joined in the conversation having a lot to say. Sarah was surprised to see her so talkative. However, after Sarah saw Mercy dancing with Dan at the wedding, she suspected that something was going on between them. And this evening when she saw the two of them get up to leave her house together; Sarah was certain that Mercy had finally snagged Dan, the love of her life.

As Dan walked Mercy home, he told her how sorry he was about what happened that night after the wedding, and asked for her forgiveness. She had gotten over what had happened, and now she was feeling overjoyed just to have him walk down the street with her. She thought to herself, "If that's what it took to get him, it was worth it." Without any hesitation she accepted his apology. He asked her if she would go to the movies with him. She said that she would be more than delighted, but asked him not to come to her house to pick her up. She said that she would meet him at Sarah's house. When they reached her front door, after they said "goodnight," he kissed her on the cheek. His lips felt so soft, she could only imagine what it was going to feel like when they really kissed. She couldn't wait to see him again.

Mercy knew that her mother would not approve of her going out with Dan. The main reason being that he was a full grown man, and she was just a young girl still in her teens. She was sure that her mother would not understand what a man his age would want from a child. Her mother also did not like the way he hung out on the corner every evening like he was up to no good. And like everyone in the neighborhood, her mother had heard he was a womanizer.

In order to go out with Dan, Mercy knew that

she would have to lie to her mother and say that she was going out with Sarah. Not that her mother liked Sarah any better. Her mother really didn't approve of any of her friends. Her mother could not understand why she would want to be with a group of people who were known to be unchurched and had the reputation of being on the wild side. She was sure that she had raised her daughter better than this. Still Sarah was Mercy's best friend, and since Sarah was a girl, she was the only person Mercy could say that she was going out with. So the day of Mercy's date with Dan, she asked her mother if she could go to the movies with Sarah. Her mother was well aware of all the times she was at Sarah's house, and the times they went places together without asking her for permission. Although her mother wondered why she asked for permission now, her mother felt there was no need for her to tell her that she couldn't go, because she probably would go to the movies with Sarah anyway. Except to keep Mercy pinned up in the house, there was no way to stop her. Her mother should have been suspicious seeing Mercy, like never before, spending so much time dressing. But she paid her daughter no attention thinking that Mercy was getting older and more conscious of her appearance.

As planned, Dan picked Mercy up at Sarah's house, and took her downtown by taxi cab to a major theatre to see a movie premiere, with top stars and Academy Award winners. If he was trying to impress her, she wasn't—he could have saved his money. As far as she was concerned they could have walked to a neighborhood theatre to see a low rated show with no known actors and actresses. She really wasn't interested in seeing any movie, she just wanted to be with him, and it didn't matter where. She was completely satisfied, and happy to spend the entire time in the dark theatre with him. Neither one paid any attention to what was on the screen. If anyone asked, she couldn't tell them the name of the movie they saw, what the movie was about, or the names of the stars that played in it.

The movie date made Mercy and Dan officially boyfriend and girlfriend. Still she had to keep their relationship a secret from her mother. The only way for Mercy to get out of the house to see Dan was to tell her mother that she was going out with Sarah or another friend from school. And she also had to keep her curfew which was ten o'clock on regular days and twelve o'clock on special occasions. It didn't matter what she had to do, Mercy didn't let anything stop her from seeing Dan. They saw each other almost every evening after he got off from work. When the weather was nice and warm, they went to lover's lane in the park. On the weekends when it was really hot, they went to the beach with his friends. Then sometimes they would double-date and go to the movies or out for dinner with Philip and Rachel. And when they really had nothing else to do, they went out of the neighborhood to a bar to have a few drinks. Although Mercy was under age, she never had any problems being served since she was tall and appeared to be mature and older than she was.

In September, shortly after returning to high school for Mercy's second year, she found out that she was pregnant. After missing her period for two months, she went to see the school nurse who sent her to see a gynecologist. And after examination and testing, she got the most feared results. Right away she went to tell Dan the news that he was going to be a father. At first he was speechless and then he said, "I guess we will have to get married." Mercy was devastated at the thought of "having" to get married. Dropping out of high school and getting married at the age of sixteen was not her plan. She wanted to be at least eighteen, graduated high school, and possibly have a job before getting married. However, Mercy loved Dan, wanted to marry him, and the child in her belly needed a father. She had no other choice but to get married.

Mercy knew that she had to tell her mother. But she was terrified and scared to death to face her, especially since she lied to her and had not told her that she was going out with Dan. The worst part was that her mother would know that they had sex. Crazy thoughts like running away or committing suicide came to her mind. Mercy couldn't help but remember the time when she was thirteen and had kissed a boy in the mouth and then started bleeding from her vagina. At that time she didn't know any better than to think that she was pregnant, and she was afraid to tell her mother. When she finally got the nerve to tell her mother about the bleeding, her mother simply gave her a sanitary napkin, a sanitary belt to hold it up, and told her that she had started her "period." Nothing else was said. In her family, anything to do with sex was a forbidden subject. She had to find out what this "period" was from the girl friends she hung out with.

Dan was just as afraid of Mercy's mother as she was. He knew how her mother felt about him going out with her daughter, and expected to be thrown out of the house. Needless to say, there was no way for him to avoid going with Mercy to face her, and the sooner the better.

Mercy's mother was really caught by surprise when she saw Dan come into her home with her daughter. She couldn't imagine what he wanted, and she didn't appreciate Mercy bringing him to her home, especially without her knowing in advance that he was coming. There was nothing her mother wanted to say to him. Therefore as they entered the living room, she got up and walked out. Mercy and Dan thought perhaps this was not a good time to tell her the news. Yet they knew that there was never going to be a good time to tell her mother that she was pregnant and they were planning to get married. And since there were no other family members at home, there would be no better time.

As she was more frightened than ever before, Mercy called her mother back into the room, and asked her to sit down. She came into the room, but refused to sit down. Seeing the way her mother was acting, they decided to say what they had to and get it over as soon as possible. So Mercy stood up in front of her mother, and with trembling voice said that she was pregnant and she was planning to marry Dan. Her mother didn't say a word, just threw up her hands, walked out the room and slammed the door behind her.

Mercy and Dan heard her sobbing uncontrollably for about fifteen minutes or so, and then she started crying out to the Lord, asking him over and over again what did she do wrong in raising Mercy; how could this happen to her? Mercy really felt bad that she had caused her mother so much grief and pain. She wanted to go into the room to give her mother a big hug and kiss, and let her know that everything was going to be alright. But Mercy knew better not to do that, remembering the last time she tried to hug her mother, she pushed her away. Her family did not display this kind of affection. So Mercy decided that it was best for her to wait in the living room with Dan until her mother came out to talk with them.

Finally Mercy's mother came back into the room. Her eyes were red and swollen from crying so hard, but it seemed that she wasn't as angry as she was before, and was now ready to sit down and talk with Mercy and Dan about their wedding plans. They had planned to marry the next month at Mt. Zion Baptist Church, the church she had attended most of her life. Since Mercy was only sixteen, they asked her mother to go with them to the license bureau to sign the papers to give her daughter permission to marry. Her mother felt that she had no other choice. She knew if she did not give Mercy permission to marry, she would have to send her down south to have the baby in secret and put the baby up for adoption. That is how it was done in those days—having a child out of wedlock was a sin and brought disgrace to the family, and Mercy could not live with the stigma.

The marriage ceremony took place in an office at Mt. Zion, and Mercy's pastor, Rev. Benjamin Moore, officiated. In no way was it like Philip's and Rachel's wedding. Sadly, she was not the bride of her dreams. She could not wear the traditional white wedding dress and veil. Since she was no longer a virgin, she had to wear an off-white, plain satin ankle length dress that was big enough to hide her pregnancy, with an off-white pill box hat on her head, and a small bunch of flowers in her glove covered hands. Mercy was a child bride trying her best to look like a woman.

The only people in attendance were Mercy's mother, father, and sisters, along with her best friend, Sarah and her best friend's brother, Philip as witnesses. No one in Dan's family came to the ceremony or to the reception held at her parent's home. His family let it be known that they wanted to be no part of this marriage. From the day they got married, it was clear that his family did not like her. Why? Mercy could not understand. To her knowledge, she had never done anything to them. Perhaps Dan's parents thought that she tricked their son into marriage; if they only knew the truth. Besides, in the same way his parents did not like her, her parents did not like him.

Usually a wedding was a day for families to come together in celebration. However, this was one of the saddest days of her life. There were more tears than laughter; it was more like a funeral, like someone had died. Mercy felt like she was the one who died—her life was over. Her aunt spoke to her in truth saying, "Your wings are clipped and you can no longer fly." Dan's wings were also clipped. At the marriage ceremony and at the reception, Mercy could see that he was unhappy. She also noticed how he went outside a couple of times with Philip. She knew that they were going out to smoke marijuana, and by evening the two of them were high as a kite and feeling no pain. Philip's wife, Rachel also knew what they had been up to, and took her husband home before he could embarrass her. Mercy wished that she had done the same when she saw how Dan, hardly able to stand up, was walking around with a foolish grin on his face.

There was no honeymoon. Mercy and Dan spent their first night in a rooming house. He did not carry her over the threshold, but stumbled ahead of her, unlocked the doors, went into their room, and fell across the bed talking about how tired he was. Still Mercy was determined to make this the romantic night that she had dreamed about. While Dan laid on the bed passed out, she went down the hall to the shared bathroom to take a shower, rub her body down with perfumed oils and put on the white satin night grown that she had purchased for the occasion. In pregnancy she had gained weight that made her body larger and gave her fuller breast. Feeling sexy, she returned to their room making a grand entrance. However, he never noticed her. He was snoring, deep in sleep still dressed in his suit, socks and shoes. There was none of the intimate love making that she had imagined for their honeymoon night. Feeling disappointed and hurt, she pushed him to the side, climbed into the bed, got under the covers and cried herself to sleep.

When people tried to tell Mercy that Dan didn't really love her, that he was only getting married to keep from going to jail, she didn't want to hear it. Now she had to accept the truth. He was guilty of statutory rape and would have had to spend time behind bars if he had been reported to the authorities. Without a doubt her parent's would have done just that. It was definitely a "shot gun" wedding. However, Mercy was still in love with Dan and she was going to try to make the best of their marriage.

With a baby on the way, Mercy knew that she had to grow up fast, put her feelings aside and be the responsible person in the household. In no way was she going to bring a baby into a rooming house with a shared bathroom and kitchen. During the first week of their marriage, she applied for Public Housing. Since Dan had worked several years as a factory worker and was receiving high wages, they were accepted for a high income City Housing Project. Within a few months they moved into their first apartment located in an integrated neighborhood across the street from a park with beautiful flowers and trees. It was a perfect place to raise a child. She imagined how she would stroll through the park with her baby in a coach carriage, the finest carriage she could buy. For the first time she was excited about having a baby. She couldn't wait for her nine months to be up.

Mercy decided that she was going to be a perfect housewife and mother, modeling her family after the television show, "Father Knows Best." In this way she could escape from her painful reality by playing house. Therefore, she kept everything in the household under control and in order. She enjoyed purchasing furniture and decorating their apartment according to the Good Housekeeping Magazine. Their apartment was picture perfect. She washed and ironed Dan's clothes; prepared meals, baked biscuits, cakes and pies according to cookbook recipes. Dinner was ready when Dan came home from work; and they sat down at the table together to eat. While Dan continued to wear tailored made suits, expensive shoes, leather coats, and jewelry, Mercy wore maternity dresses when she was pregnant, cotton house dresses and aprons when she was not, and she wore cheap plastic shoes and cloth coats. Mercy loved her husband.

However, clipped wings certainly did not stop Dan from flying the coup and hanging out as he did before the marriage. He would get up early on Saturday mornings to press his clothes, shine his shoes and jewelry, manicure his nails, bathe and rub his body down in lotion and sweet smelling cologne. By evening he would be dressed sharp as a tack. Giving her a quick kiss on the cheek, he would head for the door saying that he was going to get a haircut and hang out with the guys for a while. Mercy knew better. Dan would come home at daylight on Sunday mornings high as a kite, hardly able to stand on his own two feet. She would help him undress, put him in the bed and climb in the bed next to him. Just because he was married didn't stop him from seeing other women. And from rumors she heard that he was seeing a lot of women, young and old, and even one of her so-called friends. She also heard that one of the women was pregnant at the same time she was. Certainly Mercy was deeply hurt when she heard these rumors. However she got satisfaction knowing that she won Dan's hand in marriage while the other women only had him on the side.

Exactly nine months from the day of Philip's and Rachel's wedding, Mercy woke up in the middle of the night having labor pains. Almost in a state of panic, she and Dan dressed as quickly as they could, called a cab and was rushed to the hospital. She had never before experienced such excruciating pains. She felt like she was going to die. For what seemed to her like hours, she screamed and hollered, tossed and turned, and broke out in a sweat all over her body. And then feeling like she was having a bowel movement, she started grunting as she pushed and pushed until she found herself in a pool of water. This time when she hollered out for help, the nurse and the doctor came running to her bedside, and with one loud scream and one hard push, she saw the baby coming from her. Suddenly she was overcome with euphoria. Her pain and screams turned into shouts of joy and thanksgiving to God. She felt blessed to have experienced the miracle of giving birth to a healthy, beautiful seven pound baby girl. Dan was a proud father, and came to the hospital daily to see her and the baby. She thought now that they had a child he would settle down to become a faithful husband and family man.

On the day Mercy was discharged from the hospital, Dan came to take her and the newborn baby home. However, before going home, they made a stop at his parent's home for his family to see the baby. Dan was greeted at the door by his family with warm kisses and hugs while his mother took the baby from Mercy's arms with a cold polite greeting. As they walked down the hall to the living room, Mercy noticed three babies, less than a month to not quite two years old, on his mother's bed. At first, she thought perhaps his mother was running a nursery. But then she almost fell off her feet when she was told that the babies were Dan's mother's grandchildren and he was their father. Mercy could barely hold back her tears as she watched his mother appearing to be happy to have another baby to care for, while Dan displayed no guilt or shame. Looking over his children on the bed, as if to show-off his accomplishments, he proudly laid his newborn baby next to them.

Mercy suspected that he was seeing other women, but she certainly did not expect him to have other children. She felt totally betrayed and so deeply hurt, like someone punched her in the pit of her stomach. She couldn't believe that Dan would treat her with no respect and no regard for her feelings. Of course he knew that his mother was taking care of his children. The question was why did he bring her to his mother's house at this time? She thought perhaps he was tired of keeping his other children a secret. But then she was amazed how he kept these babies and their mothers a secret when, she was sure, he had to pay child support. Mercy wished that she could take her baby and run far away from Dan and his family. But she was trapped in a situation that she could not get out.

When they arrived home, Mercy questioned Dan about the children and their mothers. He simply said that he was involved with these women before her time, and that was the end of the conversation. Dan did not need to say anything else; she could see for herself, everything people said about him was true. There was no longer any doubt in Mercy's mind that Dan married her because he had to, and if he could have gotten away without marrying her as he did the other women, he would still be a single man with no strings attached. However, Mercy decided that she was not going to give up no matter what he did, she was staying with Dan.

He turned out to be a good father. He changed diapers, fed the baby the bottle, and got up in the middle of the night when the baby cried. Dan even gave Mercy more attention, and their life together became more romantic. Not knowing about the use of birth control pills, it seemed that she stayed pregnant. She had heard that some men believe "the best way to keep a wife was to keep her barefoot and pregnant." Although she had shoes on her feet, Mercy was beginning to believe that Dan was surely trying to keep her pregnant. However, after having four children she said enough. When she heard about Planned Parenthood, she decided to go there for help as soon as possible.

Mercy loved her children and tried to give them the things that she wished she had as a child. She was determined not to deprive them of love and affection in the way she was. Every chance she had, she was hugging and kissing her children, and she did not believe in punishing a child with a strap but found positive methods to discipline them. She enjoyed dressing her children up and learned how to sew so that she could make their clothing.

There was never any doubt that Dan loved his children. He worked hard to provide for his family so that Mercy could take the children ice skating and roller skating, on trips to the zoo, to amusement parks, to the beach, to children shows, to the circus, to parades, to the library, and museums. Sometimes Dan would go with them on these trips, and on picnics and summer vacations. The children had birthday parties, graduation parties, and parties just to party. The girls had dancing lessons, and when they were old enough they participated in the cotillion. The boys belonged to the boy scouts, and the girls belonged to the girl scouts. During the Christmas season they went to see Santa Claus, had the biggest Christmas tree that their father could find, received lots of gifts and more toys than they could play with. When the City Housing Project apartment became too small for the family, they moved to a private house in the suburbs so that the children could have a basement and a backyard to play in.

Dan was not a Christian man and called Mercy a religious fanatic. He only went to church for baby dedications, funerals and weddings. With or without him, she was determined that she was going to raise her children in church in the way she was. Therefore, she took her children to church on Sundays, and they attended Sunday school and participated in the church programs. Their children grew up to be well mannered, respected themselves and others, didn't get into any trouble, didn't use drugs, stayed out of jail, finished high school and got good paying jobs.

Only God could have saved their children from Mercy's madness. Keeping the house clean and everything in order was her only strict rule. The children could not put their hands on the walls or bring toys out of their rooms; they had to pick up after themselves, stay out of the living room, and eat at the table. When people came to visit they would wonder how she kept her house so clean with four children. Their compliments about her housekeeping made her feel very proud. And that's what she needed. Mercy was trying her best to be a perfect mother with perfect children. Trying to accomplish this and at the same time please Dan almost drove her insane.

As Mercy grew older it became obvious that she and Dan had very little in common. He loved to play ball, watch sports on the television or go to the games, go fishing, play cards and hang out with his friends. She took no part in these activities. They rarely did anything together. She went her way and he went his. As the years went by, they grew further and further apart and she began to fall out of love with him. They lived in the same house as roommates, only staying together for the sake of the children.

Finally it came to the point when Dan was bringing women to their home while she was out. One evening Mercy and the children came home unexpectedly, and found Dan and a woman on the sofa having drinks. The woman was surprised to see her, and jumped up and ran out the house as fast as she could. In his cool manner, he got up off the sofa and walked out the room saying, "We weren't doing anything wrong," and acted as if she was the one who had done something wrong. Dan might as well had said, "Go on and believe your lying eyes." Indeed, this was the last straw. Mercy felt like killing him.

Over the years Dan had caused her a lot of pain and suffering. Too many nights Mercy cried herself to sleep. She had enough and made up her mind that she was not going to let him hurt her anymore. He wasn't worth it. She had outgrown him, and found him to be shallow. All he had going for himself was the clothes on his back, a few dollars in his pocket, and not a dime in the bank. And he was forever "waiting for his ship to come in" although he never sent one out.

For comfort, Mercy turned to alcohol. At first it was just a can of beer in the morning to get her going. When that was not enough, she would drink two beers, then three beers, and finally a six pack a day. When beer alone no longer did the trick, she turned to drinking hard core whiskey daily. She would drink whatever she could afford or whatever anyone offered her, it didn't matter the brand. There was always a glass in one hand and a cigarette in the other.

Mercy's playing house days were over. She got rid of her house dresses, aprons, plastic shoes and cloth coats, and looked in fashion magazines for the latest fashions. Clothes she couldn't afford to buy, she made herself. She had her hair dyed blond, got a stylish hair cut, and learned how to put on makeup. Mercy looked into the mirror and was amazed to see how she had grown up to be so beautiful. She felt like a new woman. Dan could not help but notice how beautiful she was and how much she had changed. He started paying her more attention and gave her compliments.

Like never before, he spent more time with her, taking her out for dinner, to the movies and shows. The first time without the children, they went on vacation in the romantic Pocono Mountains. However, his show of love and affection was too late; he was no longer the love of her life. Her love for him was dead. She was ready to step out on the town. "What was good for the goose is now good for the gander," became her favorite saying. If Dan could dress up and hang out with his friends, Mercy made up her mind that she was going to do the same.

CHAPTER 2
Friends and Lovers

It was not long before Mercy met some new friends to hang out with. One day while she was standing on line at the supermarket check-out counter, an attractive woman started a conversation with her. The woman said that her name was Jezebel, but people called her Jazzy. After they paid for their groceries and were off the line, Jazzy took Mercy aside to tell her about a women's social club and invited her to one of their luncheon meetings. Mercy was looking forward to having some place to go, and accepted the invitation not knowing anything about the social club or its members.

Mercy felt safe going to the luncheon meeting since it was held at Jazzy home and she appeared to be friendly and was not a complete stranger. When she arrived at the meeting she was warmly greeted by four very friendly attractive women who made her feel welcome. She could see the women were drinking, there was no food insight, and they were slightly intoxicated at one o'clock in the afternoon. Jazzy offered her a drink of scotch and soda, and immediately Mercy felt that she was in the right place with like-minded women.

The social club turned out to be a group of lonely, love starved suburban housewives who met to talk about their children, husbands, the other men in their lives, and make plans for the weekend. All the women had male lovers, and sometimes they would hang-out and drink at one of the male lovers' home or they would go solo to the city and hang-out in the bars. The owners of the bars and the bartenders were delighted to see them coming because they lit up the place and were good for business. These attractive women could attract men like bees to honey. They were the fabulous five, and were treated like royalty. When they entered a bar, the men would jump up off their bar stools to give them their seats and surround them buying drinks until closing time. Mercy really enjoyed the attention the men gave them. Most often, the women would leave the bar too drunk to stand up, and they would all get in a car to be driven home by a woman who was in a stupor. It was amazing the driver was never stopped by the police and served with a DWI. Even worse, they could have been in a terrible accident and somebody could have been killed. In those times Mercy had no doubt that God was with her.

Sometimes when Mercy went out with her friends and their lovers they would hook her up with a man. Most often these were married men cheating on their wives in the same way her husband was cheating on her. Surely this was not the kind of relationship she was looking for. Being with a married man made her feel very uncomfortable as she thought about his wife at home. While her girl friends and the men they were with were having a good time drinking, laughing and talking, she would be feeling too bad to join them as her mind would be on those times when her husband stayed out all night with other women. She would recall the many nights she stayed awake worrying about where he was and what was he doing; her imaginations running wild until she would finally cry herself to sleep. In no way did she want another woman to suffer heartache and pain on her account.

None of the women were employed so they were able to get together to drink or go out whenever they wanted to. They were partners in crime, when you saw one, more than likely you would see the others. With these women it was always party time. When they were not hanging out in bars, they would have friends—men and women—over to one of their homes. In the summer time they would have cook-outs or go to the beach, and they would take their children with them. Seldom were their husbands around for these occasions. With her women friends being so attractive, Mercy knew the temptation would be too great for Dan. He would be like a fox in a hen house.

COME, SEE A MAN

Mercy could never forget the Sunday she had a cook-out in the backyard of her home. Although they really couldn't afford it, Dan liked to show off and do things in a big way. She invited all her family members, relatives, friends of the family and the women she hung out with. Everyone came and some guests brought friends with them. Needless to say the backyard was packed. It was really a grand time with music and laughter filling the air. All day and into the night the guests ate hot dogs, hamburgers, chicken and spareribs straight off the grill. And they piled their plates with potato salad, Cole slaw, corn-on-the-cob, baked beans, cakes and pies. There was more than enough food. And when the day started with all kinds of alcohol beverages including a keg of beer, there was more than enough to drink. However, by evening all the alcohol was gone and everyone was visibly high. And yet they were looking for more to drink.

As far as Mercy was concerned, the guests had enough of everything and it was time for them to go home. But Dan didn't want to hear that. In spite of the fact that he could not afford to buy anything else, he insisted on going out to find some more to drink. Being that it was Sunday, he would have to go to an after-hour spot where they sold alcohol beverages for a higher price than the liquor stores. And since he didn't own a car, he had to ask someone to take him there. Without hesitation, Jazzy volunteered. From the smile on his face, Mercy could see that he was more than happy to have Jazzy as his driver. But this did not sit well at all with Mercy. She preferred that it was a man and not a woman taking him. She did not trust her husband going out with her friend. She wished that she could have gone with them, but she could not leave her guests.

From the time Dan and Jazzy left, Mercy was nervously looking at the clock on the wall to see how long it would take them to come back. When they were gone for more than an hour, Mercy suspected that they were up to something. Every few minutes she would leave her guests and stand outside in front of the house looking for them. By this time, the guests started questioning why it was taking Dan and Jazzy so long to buy the alcohol. Mercy was never before so embarrassed, and didn't know what to say to her quests. Some of the guests got tired of waiting and left. The party was over. She wished that all of them would leave.

Two hours later, while Mercy was standing outside in front of the house, she saw Jazzy's car speeding through the block. She couldn't understand where Jazzy was going. She could not have been looking for a place to park the car since there were plenty of parking spaces in front of her house. When Mercy looked down the street and saw Jazzy's car parked on the next block, she knew that something was going on between them.

Mercy was furious as she walked down the street fuming, boiling, madder than mad. When she reached the car, she saw her husband and her friend locked up in each other's arms. They were certainly not expecting to see her; and were in shock when they saw her angry face in the car window looking at them. Mercy screamed and shouted loud enough for the whole neighborhood to hear her asking, "Would somebody please tell me what's going on?" She couldn't believe that her friend would betray her like this. Jazzy had gone against the unwritten code of ethics among friends that says "friends don't mess with friends' husbands". Lucky for her that Mercy did not a have a bat, she would have smashed out all of Jazzy's car windows. However, Mercy was not surprised at her husband because she knew the kind of man she was married to.

Dan jumped out of the car and as usual he said that they were not doing anything wrong; he was only trying to get something out of Jazzy's eye. Mercy had heard this line before and this time she was no fool. Jazzy knew that it was time for her to go home so she drove away leaving Mercy and Dan standing on the street arguing with one another. After that night, Mercy ended her friendship with Jazzy and the women of the so-called social club. It was easy for her to see how these women were friends of no one not even themselves.

Mercy felt like she didn't need them anymore. She had gone out many times with the women and now she had the courage to go out by herself. On these occasions, she would go to the bars where she was familiar and knew some of the men. Most often when the men saw her sitting at the bar alone, one of them would come to sit on the stool next to her, buying her drinks while flattering her with compliments and trying to get her telephone number or trying to take her home with him. For all she knew, the men she was drinking with could have been psychopaths, serial killers or sociopaths. She thanked God to be alive when she thought about how she could have been found dead in some dark ally. Although she knew what she was doing was very dangerous, she couldn't stop. She was obsessed with finding a drink as well as finding a man to love her.

Once in a while a man would show sincere interest in having an affair with her, and their relationship would last for several months. There was one man named Peter who seemed to honestly care for Mercy. He wore thick eyeglasses and was not at all handsome, but he was kind hearted, single, and employed as an accountant for a government agency. He rarely hung out in the bars since he kept a bar stocked with whiskey at his home. But as fate had it, one evening after work, he decided to stop for a drink at the bar on the corner where he lived. When he saw Mercy sitting at the bar all alone, he walked over to her and offered to buy her a drink. She accepted his offer, and then the two of them became engaged in conversation. She found him different from the men she usually met in the bars. He didn't flatter her with compliments, but they talked in general about what was happening in the country and how things were changing in the neighborhood.

During the course of the evening, and after a few drinks, they began to feel like old friends. Although Peter had not planned to, he ended up staying in the bar talking to Mercy until closing time. As he was leaving he asked if he could call her sometimes and perhaps they could see one another again.

It made Mercy feel good to meet a man that did not want to take her to bed the first night, and she looked forward to having a relationship with him. Mercy thought that Peter came at just the right time when she really needed a friend. She didn't want to tell him that she was married because she was afraid that would chase him away. But she felt that she had to tell him the truth. After Mercy briefly told Peter about her bad marriage, and that it would not stop her from seeing him, he wrote down his telephone number on a match book, gave it to her, and said that she could call him any time.

Mercy did not want to appear too anxious, so she waited two days before calling Peter. It seemed like he was sitting by the telephone waiting for her to call; she could hear it in his voice. He talked about how glad he was to hear from her, and he wanted to see her that evening. She agreed to see him and said that they could meet at the corner bar where they first met.

Although she was not that crazy about Peter, she was determined to hold on to him until something better came along. In order to accomplish this she knew that she had to look irresistible. So she spent the entire afternoon looking for something to wear, and washing and setting her hair. She finally decided to wear a flattering white cotton mini sundress with her silver spike heel sandals. When she finished dressing and saw herself in the mirror, she smiled with approval that she had accomplished her mission to look as irresistible as she could. And after twisting and turning in front of the mirror to admire herself, she hurried out of the house and arrived at the bar just as Peter drove up in his car. Her eyes popped when she saw him pull up to the curb in the latest model Mercedes Benz. "He's no joke," she thought to herself. She didn't wait for him to come into the bar, but ran out to meet him. He made a big deal complimenting her on how good she looked, but she did not say a word about his car since she did not want him to think that she was not used to anything.

Since it was a beautiful summer evening, Peter suggested that they drive down by the river to watch the sunset. Mercy had her reservations about going by the river to watch the sunset. She didn't trust him or any other man. However, she really had him wrong. When they arrived by the water, he pushed the steering wheel out of his way, got out of the car, went to the back seat and pulled out a traveling bar with scotch, ginger ale, ice, and cups. As he fixed their drinks, he told her how he did not like to drink by himself, how bars served watered down whiskey that was too expensive, and how glad he was to have someone to drink with.

That evening while they were sitting and drinking

by the water, Peter let her know that he never married and didn't have any children. He also talked about his past relationships that didn't work out, and he was still looking for the woman that was right for him. While Peter continued to talk about himself, Mercy learned that he was born and raised in South Carolina where both of his parents still lived with his two younger sisters. She also learned that he graduated from college with a degree in accounting. Although he was never baptized, he considered himself to be a Christian, and he didn't go to church because he believed that he could worship God at home. Mercy certainly didn't want to make him feel bad, but she felt that she had to say something about the need for him to be baptized, and worshipping God at home was not the same as worshipping in church. He agreed and said that he wasn't there yet, but when the time came he would do the right thing. Then Mercy let Peter know that she was a baptized Christian and attended church every Sunday when possible. She also talked about Mt. Zion Baptist Church and invited him to visit one Sunday. Mercy was quick to tell Peter that her husband called her a religious fanatic and never went to church, and she hoped that he would not be like her husband. She went on to talk about her failing marriage and her four children.

Mercy let Peter know that she was looking for the man who wanted to have a serious relationship with her. Peter suggested that they might be right for each other. One thing she knew for certain was that they enjoyed talking to each other. Around midnight he placed everything into his travel bar, adjusted the steering wheel, and drove her back to the bar on his corner. Before she got out of the car he made her promise that she would call him the next day.

The following day as soon as she could, Mercy gave Peter a call. He wanted to see her again that evening after work. She agreed; but this time he wanted her to come to his apartment. Still not trusting men she hesitated wondering what his motive was. He could hear fear in her voice, and her hesitation made him aware that she didn't feel comfortable coming to his apartment. To assure her that she was safe with him, he said that she could sit on the chair by the front door, and anytime she felt uncomfortable she could get up and leave; and he promised that he would not try to stop her. She was okay with this and went to his apartment that evening. He really surprised her when she arrived and he was standing outside. He said that he would prefer to wait until the time when she was ready to come inside. Since he had not had dinner, he asked if she would like to go out to have dinner and a few drinks with him. She was impressed by his consideration of her feelings, and gladly accepted his invitation to go out for dinner.

Mercy and Peter were well aware that they had to be discreet and go to places where she would not be seen by anyone she knew. Therefore, they decided not to stay in the neighborhood, but to go out to the Island to a sea food restaurant. Indeed, this was a wise choice.

She really enjoyed the sea food, and wished that she had room for seconds. But the best part of the evening was not the food, but dancing to live music, outside by the water, under the stars. When they finished their dinner, they went out on the floor and danced cheek to cheek until closing time. That did it. After dancing all evening, both Mercy and Peter were in no mood for her to go home. Therefore, without asking for her approval, he drove straight to his place.

Mercy had more than a few drinks that evening and was feeling no pain. She didn't care where he took her. When Peter opened the door to his apartment, Mercy went inside feeling in no way uncomfortable. While she was sitting on the sofa, he turned the lights down low, turned on some soft music, sat down beside her, and then took her into his arms to tell her how much he loved her. She was caught by surprise and didn't know what to say since she didn't feel the same way he did. However, in order not to hurt his feelings and also to keep him, she lied and said that she loved him also. As the night was getting late, and it was time for her to go home, he told her that there was no hurry for her to leave. When she insisted that she had to go home, he gave her his set of spare keys to visit him anytime she wanted to, and also gave her money to take a cab home.

The next day Mercy came to Peter's place before he arrived home from work. And as she looked around his apartment, she couldn't help but notice how sparsely it was furnished, and how badly the walls needed painting. In the living room he only had a sofa, a chair, a floor lamp, a portable radio and a small television set. The bedroom only had a bed, a dresser, night table and lamp. And there were only two suits, a pair of black shoes and a pair of sneakers, a few shirts, one sweater, two pairs of pants, and an overcoat in his closet. In the kitchen there were only two chairs and a table to eat on. In the kitchen cabinet she noticed that he only had a couple of dishes, and four glasses. She was really concerned when she saw one of the kitchen cabinets filled with top brands of scotch, rum, gin, bourbon, and all kinds of wine. Peter surely didn't seem like the kind of man who entertained at lot nor had visitors to come to see him and drink all this alcohol. And from the looks of things it didn't seem like he was about to have a party.

The way Peter lived told Mercy a lot about his character. She guessed that he had a drinking problem, and spent most of his money on alcohol. She had no doubt that he spent a lot of his money making car note payments for his Mercedes Benz, but he certainly did not spend much money on clothes or furniture for his apartment. At first Mercy had thought that Peter was just plain cheap, but now she could understand why he didn't like to drink in bars since he had more than enough to drink in his apartment.

As the days, weeks, and months passed, Mercy was usually at Peter's apartment when he came home from work. And instead of her being at home cooking dinner for her husband when he got off from work, she was now cooking dinner for Peter. She felt like she was playing house again. In the same way she used to clean her home, she was now cleaning Peter's apartment. She was also washing and ironing his clothes. Needless to say, Mercy really enjoyed doing these things for Peter. With all the alcohol in his kitchen cabinet, she could drink all she wanted while she was working. And it never seemed to bother Peter that Mercy was intoxicated when he arrived home. In order to catch up with her, he would just refill his glass several times with scotch on the rocks. After dinner they would usually sit in the living room holding hands and watching television until it was time for her to go home.

Once in a while Peter would take Mercy out for dinner or to see a movie. And to express his love for her, sometimes when he came home from work he would bring her a bunch of fresh roses. Peter also gave her a gold bracelet, and whenever he got paid, he would give her money to buy something special for herself.

Mercy and Peter were getting along swell. She thought that at last she found a man who really loved her. That is why it came as a terrible shock to her the evening, just before Thanksgiving when he came home from work, had a couple of drinks and dinner as usual, and then without any explanation asked her to return his keys, and said their relationship was over. She broke out in tears as she couldn't understand what she did wrong. As far as she was concerned they were getting along just fine. In all the times they were together, they never had any major arguments, and he never complained to her about anything. As she was an emotional wreck, she begged him to tell her why he didn't want her any more. Without any show of emotions, Peter told Mercy that he thought that it was best for them to break up now than go on with a relationship that had no future. He said that he wanted to get married and raise a family, and he could not do that with her since she was already married. It really made her mad when he gave that as a reason for her to leave. She really felt like slapping him in the face. He knew when they first met that she was married. If he had asked her, she might have considered leaving her husband. But he never said anything to her about getting a divorce and marrying him.

To Mercy, Peter sounded like a man who had found another woman. When she questioned him about this, he admitted that he had met someone who was single, and he wanted to spend some time to get to know her. She couldn't believe that he could fall out of love with her so fast. She thought perhaps he didn't love her in the first place—it was all a lie. Mercy left Peter's apartment that evening feeling devastated, like someone had stabbed her in the heart. Now she could see why Peter stayed single; she was sure that he wanted no attachments holding him down, preventing him from going from woman to woman. Indeed, she saw him to be no different than her husband. She went home really broken up and depressed with more reasons to get drunk.

While Mercy was spending so much time with Peter her home was falling apart. When she was home, she was usually too drunk or too depressed to clean the house or cook the way she used to, and she spent little time with the children. She was grateful that the children were old enough to care for themselves, since most of the time when she was home she was in bed with a hangover. Dan cared less about what she did or did not do. It did not bother him that she was going out so much; her going out gave him permission to do the same. Most of the time, she would be coming in while he was on his way out.

CHAPTER 3

Lost and Found

Things only got worse. Mercy stopped going to church and turned her back on God hoping that He could not see the sinful way she was living. She felt that she no longer needed Jesus. Alcohol became her friend, her all and all. Whenever she needed strength, she turned to alcohol. When she needed comfort, she turned to alcohol. When she felt depressed, she tuned to alcohol. In the beginning, alcohol worked for her. However, after a while alcohol turned on her and her life started going downhill. She stopped caring about her appearance and started going to dingy bars and hanging out with men and women who were sloppy drunks just like her. She had become promiscuous. Getting the next drink was all she cared about.

On one of these occasions Mercy met Lucifer, who became her drinking partner and needed to drink just as much as she did. Although he was a postal worker and earned good wages, he never had any money because he would drink up all he made. He was up to his neck in debt as he borrowed more money than he could ever pay back. He didn't pay any rent nor did he have any utility bills since he lived in an apartment building that was abandoned by the landlord. In his apartment there was no gas and electricity, no heat or hot water. Therefore, he didn't shave, bathe or change his clothes often. Sometimes on payday he would rent a room in a hotel in order to clean himself up. Most of the time, he looked and smelled like a dirty homeless bum. For Mercy to hang out with the likes of Lucifer only shows how low she had become. She had hit the bottom of the barrel. It didn't matter to her how bad off he was, all she wanted was another drink.

Lucifer worked downtown at the Main Post Office, sorting mail. Whenever he had the money he would purchase a pint of cheap whiskey to take with him to work, and during the day he would go into the men's room and hide in a stall to sneak a drink. By the end of the day the pint would be gone, and he would be a total wreck waiting for the next drink. As soon as he got off from work, he would head straight for the bar down the street from the Post Office. The bartender could keep time by Lucifer. Unless he took the day off, everyday at exactly five after four, Lucifer would walk through the door. Knowing how badly he would need a drink, the bartender would have a tall glass of scotch on the rocks waiting for him on the bar. Usually he did not have any money, but the owner of the bar could always count on him to pay his tab on payday.

Mercy knew that if she wanted to see Lucifer, she had better be standing in front of the Post Office waiting for him to get off from work. Therefore, whenever she wasn't too bad-off drunk or with a hangover, and could get out of bed and get dress, she would take the subway downtown. He would be happy to see her; especially on the days he didn't have any money. There were times when he didn't even have enough money to buy a token to go home. These times he would count on her to loan him a few dollars until payday. On the days Mercy didn't go downtown to meet him; he had to borrow money from one of his co-workers who were usually in the bar with him.

As long as they could hold a drink down and were feeling good, Mercy and Lucifer would stay in the bar laughing and talking until they could hardly stand up. Then they would stumble out of the bar, and falling down drunk try to make it to the subway and uptown. They were certainly one pitiful sight, but Mercy had no shame. There were times when they were so drunk that they passed out on the train and missed their stop. Still, no matter how drunk they were, they would put their money together to purchase a pint of whatever they could afford, and then go to his apartment to continue drinking by candlelight (this was in no way for the purpose of creating a romantic atmosphere). After buying the whiskey, if they had any money left, they would buy a hamburger and a bag of French Fries to split between them. Even this was more than they could eat since most of the time they felt full from eating the peanuts on the bar, and God only knows how many drinks. There was definitely no intimacy in their relationship. Sad to say, alcohol had become the love of her life. Mercy and Lucifer wanted nothing more than to drink, drink, and drink some more, until they passed out in their clothes and slept right where they were on the floor, chair or bed. In the morning when he went to work, she went home.

One morning when Mercy woke up, she decided that she was not going home, that she was going to stay and live with Lucifer. The apartment where he was staying was filthy and he was sleeping on a dirty used mattress that he found on the street. Drunk or sober she could not live in this way. So Lucifer decided that he was going to take some time off from his job to paint and clean up the apartment. That morning Mercy and Lucifer went to the hardware store to purchase the cleaning materials and some paint. On the way home, they stopped at the liquor store to purchase a pint of cheap whiskey. Their intention was to drink no more than this pint until the work was finished. Needless to say, after the first drink that morning they went on a drinking spree that lasted for a whole week. It was like they had turned on a water fountain that could not be turned off. Whenever they ran out of alcohol they would argue about who had the last drink. Sometimes these arguments really got nasty, and they would almost get into a fight. Thank God, no one ever got hurt.

All of Mercy's dreams had now turned into a nightmare. She was no longer living the lifestyle like the television show, "Father knows Best", trying to be the perfect housewife and perfect mother. Like Lucifer, Mercy had become a dirty drunk, smelling like she fell into a whiskey barrel. She neither bathe nor changed her clothes, nor combed her hair for a whole week. One night after a day of binge drinking she looked at herself in the mirror and was horrified at what she saw. She could not go on living like this. She thought about suicide. "Stop the world I want to get off" she shouted. That night she got on her knees and prayed to God, pleading for His help, like she never prayed before.

The next morning when Mercy woke up, she made up her mind to go back home. However, she was going to take one more drink before she did this. Therefore, she left Lucifer's apartment to go to the liquor store to buy one more pint of whiskey which she promised herself would be her last drink. However, something amazing came over her as she was about to enter the store. It felt like someone had put their hands her on shoulder and stopped her in her tracks. She looked around and did not see anyone. Then suddenly she had a change of mind about having that last drink. She turned away from the liquor store and walked a few blocks to the bus stop. While waiting for the bus she wondered where she was going. When the bus came, she boarded the bus, paid the fare and took a seat near a window trying to figure out which direction the bus was headed. When the bus stopped in front of a hospital, she got off the bus and went to the hospital emergency room. She felt that she had no reason to be in the hospital, much less the emergency room. She only had a headache and felt sick on the stomach from a hangover, which was a normal feeling for her. She decided that she was just going to sit down on a bench until she felt better. As soon as she sat down, she passed out.

For several hours, Mercy was out like a light. When she woke up, she noticed a sign that read, "Psychiatric Emergency." Indeed, she felt that she was losing her mind. So she decided that she would go to see a psych doctor. When she saw the doctor, she started rambling about all the things that happened to her from childhood. The doctor let her ramble on for a few minutes and then he asked her about her drinking. She was filthy dirty and reeked of alcohol, and yet she answered that she only took a drink once in a while to be social. Surely, the doctor was amused by her answer. He could easily see that she was not a social drinker, and suggested that she be admitted to the hospital's detoxification unit. She agreed to be admitted even though she was not sure what the detoxification unit was. However, she felt a few days in the hospital would do her good and then she would be ready to go back home to her family.

When Mercy got to the floor of the detoxification

unit and found that it was a locked ward, thinking that she was being admitted to the crazy house, she was ready to turn around and leave. But the nurses on the floor would not let her. During the intake when she was told that she would have to stay for two weeks, she said, "No way." As she was led to her room, she noticed other patients in a dayroom playing cards and watching television. Right away she felt that she was in the wrong place. From what Mercy could see, the people looked down and out and not like the kind of people she associated with. Although she only had two dollars in her pocketbook, she held it tightly in her hand as if someone was going to steal it. She made up her mind that she was going to stay away from these people. The people just looked at her and laughed. Indeed, she was the one who looked down and out.

After dinner that evening, two men dressed in suits came on the unit and gathered all the patients in the dayroom for a meeting. Mercy wanted to see what the meeting was all about so she went into the dayroom and sat down on the sofa in the back of the room. The men put up a poster on the wall that read "The Twelve Steps of Alcoholics Anonymous."[8] "I am no alcoholic. I got to get out of here," she said to herself as she walked out of the room. Mercy went into the nurses' station and complained that the doctor admitted her to the wrong unit. The nurse on duty suggested that she stay on the unit for the night and in the morning she could

_____
8   Alcoholics Anonymous Publishers, 1938

see about getting a transfer. Mercy agreed to do this, and went into her room and got into bed still in her dirty clothes, refusing the pajamas and clean clothes that were given to her.

After the meeting the two men came into Mercy's room and asked her why she left. She told them that she was not an alcoholic; that she was mistakenly admitted to the wrong unit. The men heard this excuse many times before, as most people when they are first admitted say this, however after clearing up they usually knew that they were in the right place. So they paid no attention to what she was saying, but introduced themselves saying that they were alcoholics, gave their names as Mark and Luke, and suggested that she come to the next meeting and just listen. Mercy could not help but notice how Mark was built like a stallion, and with his clean shaven head and diamond post in his ear, he looked like the movie star Yule Brenner. She certainly wanted to see him again. However, she refused their invitation and said that she would not be at the next meeting since she was going to be transferred to another unit. Mark and Luke just smiled, said "Ok" and left. After tossing and turning in bed most of night, Mercy went to the nurses' station and asked for something to help her to sleep. The nurse gave her some pills that knocked her out.

The next day Mercy felt too sick to get out of bed. She just slept most of the day and did not have a desire to eat anything. That evening, the nurse convinced her that she would feel better if she took a shower and changed her clothes. There was no question about it, she definitely needed a shower. And just as the nurse said, the warm water from the shower beating against her body was really refreshing. After having a cup of warm chicken soup, Mercy got into bed that night and didn't need any medication to help her sleep. In the middle of the night she woke up as her body suddenly started shaking uncontrollably. She felt like she was experiencing an exorcism. Almost frighten to death, she called out for help and the nurse came running into her room to see what was wrong. When the nurse saw what was happening to her, the nurse did not seem surprised, but gave her some more pills to calm her down.

The next morning when Mercy woke up, she felt a change had come over her, and forgot all about being transferred to another unit. After a quick shower, she bushed her teeth, combed her hair and got dressed in the jeans and polo shirt the nurse gave her; then she went into the dayroom to have breakfast. No one was surprise to see how her attitude had changed. All the patients had been there and done that. One of the women in the room offered her a cigarette then offered to make her a cup of coffee. Mercy accepted the woman's offer, and when she returned with the cup of coffee, she sat down in the chair next to Mercy saying that her name was Deborah. Shaking like a leaf, Mercy took the cup of coffee and was embarrassed when she almost spilled the hot coffee on the woman. This didn't seem to bother Deborah, and everyone was so friendly, going out of their way to make her feel like she was one of them. And that was okay with her. Realizing how crazy she must have looked on the day when she was admitted, she could no longer look down on the patients. She was just so happy to be in their company and stayed in the dayroom the entire day watching television and playing cards. It had been so long ago, she couldn't remember when she felt so good and relaxed without having a drink.

That evening after dinner two women, Mary and Rebecca, came to lead the AA meeting. As the leaders went around to each person in the room, along with their first name, everyone admitted that they were an alcoholic and said a few words about their drinking. When Mercy's turn came, she was so nervous and shaking so badly she could hardly open her mouth. After taking a deep breath, she shouted out her first name and that she was an alcoholic so loudly that everyone in the room turned around and looked at her. At first she was embarrassed, but then she lowered her voice to say a few words about her drinking. When she finished speaking it felt like a ton of bricks was lifted off her shoulders. Never before in her life had Mercy felt so free. Her wings were no longer clipped.

When the AA meeting was over, Mercy went back to her room and laid across the bed thinking about the day she came to the hospital. All of a sudden it hit her like a bolt of lightning: the hands that stopped her from going into the liquor store to buy a pint of whiskey that morning were the hands of Jesus. She thought about the Bible story of Paul's conversion experience on the road to Damascus.[9] Surely Jesus had stopped her on the road to destruction. Mercy knew that she was saved by Jesus; she had no doubt in her mind that she also had a conversion experience. She knew that it was Jesus who met her in front of the liquor store and led her to the hospital's detoxification unit.

Mercy then thought about the Bible story of the "Lost Son,"[10] who left home and spent all of his possessions on wild living, and ended up in a pig's pen almost starving to death. Finally, he came to his senses and decided to go back home. While he still had a long ways to go before reaching home, his father saw him and ran out to meet him; filled with compassion, he took his son in his arms and kissed him. The father dressed his son in a fine robe, put a ring on his finger and sandals on his feet, and held a big feast to celebrate his lost son's return. When Mercy realized how much her story was like the "Lost Son," she fell to her knees thanking and praising God for giving her a second chance in life, and began singing in a loud voice,

"Amazing grace how sweet the sound that saved a wretch like me!

I once was lost but now am found. Was blind but now I see."[11]

Indeed, there was no doubt in her mind that it was not for any good that she had done; but she was saved by the grace of God.

---

9   Acts 9:3-19

10   Luke 15:1-31

11   John Newton, Amazing Grace

Mercy also came to realize that we have "a got you God": once you turn your life over to God, no matter how far you stray, He will never leave you or let you go. She found it to be true, you can't hide from God. She thought about the times when she was out there drinking, there were many times, many places, and many situations where she could have ended up dead. But now she could see how God was always with her, to protect her from all harm and danger, in the way the Psalmist wrote[12]:

"Where can I go from your Spirit?
where I flee from your presence?
If I go up to the heavens,
     you are there;
if I make my bed in the depths,
     you are there.
If I rise on the wings of the dawn,
if I settle on the far side of the sea,
even there your hand will guide me,
your right hand will hold me fast.

Although Mercy was raised in the church and was baptized at the age of thirteen, she had never fully accepted Jesus Christ as her Lord and Savior. He was the God of the Bible and of her parents; she did not know Him for herself. Now that she had experienced Him personally for herself, she became a true believer and was ready to turn her life completely over to Him.

---

12   Psalm 139: 7-10

She left the hospital a new person in Christ Jesus, and began to change spiritually and mentally; she no longer felt the same way about things. However, Mercy was aware that she was child-like with a lot of growing up to do.

Mercy stayed in the hospital's detoxification unit for two weeks, attending AA meetings every evening and sharing her story. While hanging out in the day room participating in group discussions, watching television and playing cards, she got to know most of the women and some of the men. They exchanged telephone numbers, made a commitment to stay in contact with one another, and attend meetings together.

CHAPTER 4
A New Beginning

Upon Mercy's discharge from the hospital, she went back home. Her children, along with Dan, met her at the door with tears and laughter, hugs and kisses. This was not what she expected. She was almost afraid to go home, expecting that her family would be angry at her for staying away and not letting anyone know where she was. Indeed, Mercy breathed a sigh of relief when she saw how happy they were to see her. Before she could get into the house and sit down, with everyone talking at the same time, they started telling her how all the family members, including her parents, called everyone she ever knew, searched all over town for weeks and they could not find her. They even notified the police and filed a missing person's report. And since no one had seen or heard from her, Dan and the children feared that they would never see her again, that she was never going to come back home, or even worse, that she was somewhere dead. Upon hearing these things, Mercy felt terribly bad and could only imagine how much grief she caused her family. She begged for their forgiveness, and then broke down in tears.

Mercy was most surprised when Dan took her in his arms and kissed her like he had never kissed her before. In the way he was behaving, and how it was written all over his face, she could see how much he feared that he had lost her. In all their years together, he had never expressed any real emotional feelings for her. In the past, he was so busy doing his thing he seemed to care less whether she was at home or not. Mercy didn't mean to hurt anyone, however, she felt that it was good for Dan to miss her this way. She thought that it was good to put some fear in him; perhaps this would cause him to change his behavior and appreciate her more.

Although Mercy was away from home for three weeks, it seemed to her more like years. In fact, this was quite true, she was gone for years. She left home years ago when she started drinking since most of the time she was so drunk it was like she wasn't there. Now that she was sober, she felt like a stranger in her own home. She sat in a chair in the living room afraid to move, not knowing what to do with her hands or how to behave without a glass in one hand and a cigarette in the other. Seeing how the children looked uncomfortable sitting and staring at her, not saying a word, she decided to go in the bathroom to take a shower so she could be alone.

That evening Dan cooked a special meal, and for the first time in a long while, the family sat down at the dinner table together. Other than Mercy giving thanks for the food, no one said a word. It was like they were afraid to speak; as if they might say something wrong. Knowing that they wanted to question her about where she had been, Mercy broke the silence telling them about her drinking problem, and how alcohol consumed her to the point where the only thing she cared about was getting the next drink. Tears swelled up in her children's eyes as she told them how alcohol led to her loss of self-respect, and to do things that she was too ashamed to talk about. Seeing the children so hurt, she broke down in tears as she told them how sorry she was to have left them and caused them so much pain. Dan also became very emotional while telling her how sorry he was to have treated her so badly, how things at home was going to be different, and how he was going to treat her better. When she told the family how she prayed and was saved by Jesus and led by Him to the hospital detoxification unit, everyone dried their tears and thanked God for bringing her back home.

Everyone's tears turned to laughter until Mercy told them that she was an alcoholic and was going to join Alcoholic Anonymous. In no way could the children or Dan accept her being an alcoholic. To them, an alcoholic was a stumbling, drunken bum out on the streets. The children refused to see their mother in this way. They all agreed that sometimes she drank too much, but she was not an alcoholic. Dan and the children talked about how they could help her control her drinking, that she had no need to go to AA. They felt that her being around this low class of people would only make her drink more. Indeed, like most people, her family had a stereotype view of an alcoholic. Therefore, she allowed them to express their feelings about AA without trying to convince them of anything different, and was sure they would understand in time.

After dinner Dan accompanied Mercy to her first AA meeting. He wanted to see what AA was all about. It was an open meeting where non-alcoholics could attend. The meeting was held in the cafeteria of a neighborhood catholic church. Both Mercy and Dan were caught by surprise when they walked into the smoke filled room and saw a large crowd of men and women standing around in groups with a coffee cup in one hand and a cigarette in the other. Everyone was well dressed, talking and laughing as if they were at a party, with no one fitting her family's description of an alcoholic. If anyone stood out looking like an alcoholic, it was Mercy and a few other newcomers who were standing alone and appearing to be lost in a fog.

The meeting was called to order by an elderly woman who looked like someone's grandmother. The room immediately got quiet and everyone took a seat. After the preliminary announcements and introductions, the speaker went to podium, and taking the mike said his first name only and that he was an alcoholic. Mercy hoped that Dan did not see her mouth fly open, and how she almost fell off her seat as she listened attentively to this very charming and handsome man tell his story of how he got drunk, used drugs, and ended up in prison for burglary before coming to AA ten years ago. She was impressed by the way he spoke so intelligently, like an important business man who had earned a college degree. She certainly did not expect to find this kind of man in AA. Indeed, she had never met a man like him in none of the bars or places where she hung out.

At the close of the meeting, the members walked around the room to speak to the new comers, exchanged telephone numbers, gave them a meeting list, and encouraged them to go to a meeting every day. Some of the members even offered to come to her home and take her to a meeting. She had never before met a group of people so friendly. In the crowd, she saw Mark and Luke standing in the middle of a group of people. Mark was looking just as fine as when Mercy first saw him. And she could see how he was so charismatic that men as well as women were drawn to him. She felt that it was no need for her to try to speak to him since he most likely would not even remember her. Being certain that she would see him again, she decided that it would be best for her to wait until the next time. From this first meeting, she felt that AA was the best thing that ever happened to her.

After the AA meeting, as Mercy and Dan were riding home in the back seat of a taxi cab, he began kissing her with passion. Indeed, she had never seen him show so much affection. However, she was in no mood for making love. It had been a long day, she was tired, and all she wanted to do was to get into bed and go to sleep. When they arrived home, he went straight into the bedroom, waiting for her to join him. Knowing what he had in mind, she took her time undressing, and put on a pair of flannel pajamas, hoping that he would get the message. When she finally got into bed, he took her into his arms in the way that she had imagined he would on their honeymoon night, twenty-two years ago. However, his show of love for her now was too late. She gently moved his arms from around her, turned over in the bed, closed her eyes and went to sleep.

After that night, Dan stopped trying to win back Mercy's love. And everyone in her family started treating her like she had some kind of terminal mental illness after they learned that alcoholism is an incurable disease. They got rid of everything in the house that contained alcohol, and tip toed around her on eggshells to prevent her from feeling any stress or tension, less she would start drinking again. They handled her with kid gloves, giving her special care and attention as if she could fall apart at any moment. Dan and the children cooked all the meals, cleaned the house and washed the clothes. The family's main concern was for her to get better. All she had to do was eat, sleep, and go to AA meetings.

Mercy learned that Mark and Luke were among the alcoholics who returned to school and studied to become drug counselors. They were now certified and worked for the government at a drug rehabilitation center. She was told that in the evenings Luke drove a school bus and went around picking up new comers and taking them to AA meetings. And sure enough, the next day after attending her first meeting, Mercy received a telephone call from Luke asking her if it would be alright for him to pick her up that evening to take her to a meeting. Of course she said that it would be alright. She was so excited to have someone like Luke give her a call, and was coming to take her to a meeting. All that afternoon, she went through her closet looking for something special to wear that evening.

Right on time Mercy was ready and sitting down waiting for Luke to arrive. As soon as he drove up to her door and blew his horn, she ran out to board the school bus. And like kids on the first day of school, everyone on the bus shouted out her name as they were so happy to see her; they were all the people she met while on the detoxification unit. As they were told to make ninety meetings in ninety days, Luke drove the school bus to pick up the new comers every evening during the week, and every Saturday and Sunday afternoon to take them to a meeting. While riding on the bus, they behaved like children, laughing, singing and playing. Mercy enjoyed being a child again, and didn't care if she never grew up. And the thought of looking for a man in AA was soon forgotten as the members showed little interest in getting emotionally involved; their only interest was staying sober.

Most of the newcomers were hard core alcoholics, drug addicts, and ex-convicts, some were homeless, and some were mentally ill. Before coming to AA, she would not dare associate with the people she used to call "low life." It did not matter now, she was one of them, and they were her best friends. Sometimes after meetings they would go to a coffee shop, or go to a movie, or go roller skating. And sometimes they would go to a members' home to play cards or to a social gathering. On occasions, she would even invite some members to her home, and they would be welcomed by her family. Indeed, she never believed that she could have so much fun sober. But then she realized that AA members were used to getting high on the spirit of alcohol, and now they are getting high on the Spirit of God.

AA does not claim to be a religious organization, but a spiritual fellowship where the members turn their lives over to the care of God. Mercy knew without a doubt that there was no way she could live without God, and took this part of the program very serious, doing whatever she could to have a closer and deeper relationship with Him. She started and ended every day on her knees in prayer, and also went to God in prayer whenever she had a need to. She read the

Bible and other inspirational literature daily. And any evening when she was not at an AA meeting she was attending an activity at Mt. Zion including prayer services and Bible Study. Every Sunday morning she taught the adult Sunday school class and attended afternoon worship services at her home church and was also a visitor at other churches.

As time went by, Mercy became deeply involved in AA and learned how to practice the Twelve Step Program. Besides attending meetings daily, she went on speaking engagements to carry the AA message at group meetings, hospitals and other institutions. She also attended AA conferences, conventions, retreats and celebrations, often traveling out of town to different cities and states. All AA groups celebrated anniversaries with special speakers, food and dancing. Mercy looked forward to attending these events and danced like she never danced before. Who would ever believe that in sobriety Mercy would become a social butterfly? Certainly, the people who were not in AA could learn from AA members how to live life.

Clearly, Mercy was spending more time out of the house sober than she did when she was drinking. However, her children had now grown to be young adults with jobs and their own interest. They were very proud of the way their mother had changed to become a better person, and the work she was doing in AA and the church. On the other hand, it appeared that Dan would rather see her drunk than sober. He had gone back to having affairs with other women and staying out all night. When she was drinking, most of the time she was passed out drunk at home or out in the street somewhere and he could come and go as he pleased without making any excuses. Now that she was sober he had a hard time doing this.

Mercy had enough of Dan's philandering ways, and made up her mind that she was not going to take it anymore. So she decided that it was time for him to go. When he stayed out all night on New Year's Eve, and didn't come home until late afternoon New Year's Day, she made a resolution to get rid of everything negative in her life that could get in the way of her mental and spiritual growth. That evening while Dan was relaxing in bed drinking a cup of coffee and reading the daily newspaper, she walked into the room and quietly told him that she wanted him to leave. He didn't act a bit surprised, but saw her asking him to leave as giving him permission to go out and stay for a few days. As quickly as he could, before she changed her mind, he jumped out of bed, got dress, took a change of clothes and left the house. He had in mind to give her time to cool off, and then he would return home.

At last, after over twenty-three years of taking Dan's emotional abuse, Mercy got the courage to file for a divorce. Early the next morning, she got out of bed, dressed, and before breakfast, she went straight to the hardware store to have her house door locks changed before Dan came back home. Then she went to see an attorney. Since her husband had left home she was able to claim abandonment and the divorce came easy. At last she was a free woman, and her husband was free to have all the women he desired.

CHAPTER 5

Her Knight In Shining Armor

One Sunday during the worship service at Mt Zion Baptist Church offering collection, a male usher passing his tray down the aisle Mercy was sitting in, made her feel very uncomfortable as he was staring at her so hard. She turned her head, not to look his way, so he would not see that she was paying attention to him. After the service, as she was walking out of the Church, she noticed that he was standing out front like he was waiting for someone. Again, she paid him no attention. However, he walked over to her and introduced himself as John Adams and asked her to forgive him for being so rude to stare so hard; that he could not help but notice that she was such an attractive woman, and he wanted to meet her. It really made Mercy feel good that he found her to be attractive, and since he seemed innocent enough she accepted his apology and told him her name. Then he added that he was a friend of Bill W.,[13] and he had noticed her before at an AA meeting. Having attended so many meetings, she could not place where she had seen him before today. As she was beginning to walk away, he stopped her and offered her a ride home. She accepted the invitation feeling that it was safe to ride in his car and let him take her home since he was also in the AA program.

Talking like two old friends, John and Mercy walked to the car together. When they approached the car, he walked around to the passenger side and opened the door for her. Right away she was impressed and thought that he was such a gentleman, for no one had ever opened the car door for her before. As he was driving her home, they never stopped talking; they had so much to talk about in regards to Mt. Zion and AA. When they arrived at her home, he got out of the car and came around to open the door for her. Then he asked her if he could call her sometimes and perhaps take her out on a date. She gave him her telephone number and said that she would like to go out with him.

That evening, Mercy could not think about anything else but John. Not that she found him to be all that attractive, but it was something about him that was holding her attention, although she couldn't

---

13   Bill Wilson, Co-Founder Alcoholics Anonymous, 1935

quite understand what it was. Certainly he was not like any man she had ever dated before. However she was definitely turned off by his heavy weight and pot belly. It didn't matter if he was polite and courteous, in no way had she ever gone out with a fat man. Still Mercy thought that John was kind of handsome with medium brown complexion, mustache, and a few strands of dark brown wavy hair that made him look like someone from the Middle East. Although he was almost bald, he wasn't sexy looking like Mark. And from what he had on that Sunday she could easily see that he was not a sharp dresser like her ex-husband, Dan; the suit that he had on looked like he had brought it off the rack at a two-for-one sale. He wore no jewelry, except for a Timex watch on his wrist. And he drove an old used car that needed a coat of fresh paint. Mercy thought that he was either cheap or he didn't have much money. In any case, she felt that it would not be any harm to go out with John since at the time she was not dating anyone. And besides, he was Christian man that she met in the church; the kind of man her mother would like.

Since Mercy was divorced less than a year, was she ready to have a relationship with a man, was the question she asked herself and also raised with her AA sponsor. Her sponsor suggested that she needed more time. With only a year of sobriety, she was still an emotional wreck, insecure and suffered with low self-esteem. Although she had gained some weight, she was still a skinny one hundred and twenty pounds, and could not see herself as being attractive in anyway. In addition, she was receiving treatment for depression since she had not yet recovered from the emotional abuse that Dan had put her through. And in spite of the way Dan treated her so badly; there still were times when Mercy thought that she should have stayed with him. Since the age of sixteen, when she married Dan, Mercy had lived with a man and was now having a difficult time living without one. Some people say that a half-of-a-loaf is better than none; that is to say it is better to have a half of man. Now Mercy was thinking that even if she shared Dan with other women, she was his wife and had the better half. Needless to say, she did not listen to her sponsor's suggestion, but waited for John to call.

Two days went by before John called Mercy and invited her to go with him to a church that held Thursday evening prayer and meditation services. She gladly accepted the invitation thinking he certainly was different; no man had ever invited her on a date to go to church. That evening when he came for her, she was turned off when she opened her door and saw him dressed in a blue plaid cotton shirt and khaki pants that needed to be pressed, and old dirty sneakers. This certainly was not the way she was used to dressing to go to church, and felt that she was over dressed in one of her Sunday best suits. However, she did not have anything to say about the way he was dressed, and he did likewise.

On the way to the church, John talked about

the different churches he attended and how he was familiar with the different denominations. Mercy felt that he was trying to impress her with his knowledge, and so she thought it best for her not to say a word less she would show her ignorance of such things. Besides she liked the sound of his baritone voice and how he spoke with so much authority.

The prayer and meditation service was held in a small non-denominational church located in midtown. As Mercy was entering the building she could easily see the seating in the sanctuary could hold no more than two hundred people, and guessed that the attendance at the service that night would probably be no more than twenty five people, and more than likely they would primary be Caucasian. Give or take a few people she was correct in the number of those in attendance, however, they were people of all races and nationalities. From the moment Mercy and John walked into the church, she could see he was no stranger there. She was amazed at his popularity. It seemed that everyone, including the pastor, stopped to speak to him and hold him in a conversation. Even though he always introduced her and included her in whatever their discussion, she felt awkward, out of place, and was too shy to speak. She breathed a sigh of relief when the service was starting and everyone sat quietly in their seats.

The prayer and meditation service was not what Mercy expected. The pastor started the service with an opening prayer, and then a petite elderly looking woman led the people for about thirty minutes in a relaxation and deep breathing exercise. After that, the sanctuary went dark as night with the only light from a few candles and a spotlight on the pulpit which shown on the same woman who spoke with a very soft voice as she read a few inspirational poems. Then soft hypnotic wind sounds broke into the darkness as the people sat silently for an hour in meditation, listening for a word from God. But no matter how hard Mercy tried to meditate in this way, she never felt or heard a thing except for her own thoughts racing around in her head. So, instead of meditating she used the silence to pray thanking God for this experience, and acknowledged that this was another thing that she needed to learn how to do. However, after this first date, John never took her back to the church for the prayer and mediation service; although she never questioned him about this, she often wondered why.

On the way home, John stopped at a luncheonette to get something to eat. They sat at the counter, and without showing Mercy the menu or asking her what she would like, for both of them he ordered tuna fish sandwiches on rye bread with lettuce and tomato, and seltzer water to drink. She sat in silent anger and too intimidated to say that she would prefer to sit at a table, and that she had something else in mind that she wanted to eat. Then when the sandwiches came, she was embarrassed by the way he garbled down his sandwich in a couple of bites and then swallowed down his drink. Noticing that Mercy had barely touched what was before her, John asked her if there was anything wrong. But before she could get the words out of her mouth to respond to his question, he reached over and took what was left of her sandwich, and garbled it down in the same way he did his. Seeing him behave so rudely, acting like a pig, her intention was to never again go out with him to eat.

For over a month Mercy and John saw each other almost daily. During the week they went to AA meetings, and on Sundays he would come to take her to Mt Zion, after the worship service they usually went to see a movie, and then he would take her home. As Mercy was spending most of her time with John, she began to break away from the AA friends she started the program with, and she stopped speaking to her sponsor. She only went to AA meetings or went on speaking engagements when she could go with John. As much as she enjoyed attending AA conferences, retreats, and anniversaries, she would only go with John. At AA anniversaries she no longer danced as much as she used to since she only danced with John. Whenever her old friends in AA had a chance to talk with her, they would express their concerns that she was not attending enough meetings and giving up to many of the things in the program that kept her sober. Of course she didn't hear a word they were saying. Although Mercy claimed that she knew what she was doing, she behaved like someone who didn't have a mind of her own. Mercy was docile the way John wanted her to be so that he could be in control; and that was okay with her.

Mercy and John's relationship was growing stronger, yet he never showed any interest in having sex with her—not even a kiss. She thought him to be strange or maybe he was a true Christian practicing celibacy. In the past, most men that she went out with wanted to have sex on the first date; no man had ever dated her for a whole month without taking her to bed. Then one Sunday after worship service and the movie, he said that he was going to buy some Chinese take-out and they could go to his house to eat. She agreed, thinking that this was going to be the day when he take her home with him to have dinner and sex.

When John drove up to a beautiful white house with green shutters on a tree lined street and manicured lawns, Mercy couldn't believe that he lived there. As he was putting the key in the front door, she asked him if he lived in the house with his mother, or someone else. When he told her that he was the owner, she began to see him in a different light; especially when he opened the door and she saw how he decorated the living room with an Italian leather sofa and chairs, expensive looking mahogany tables, crystals lamps, original paintings, thick wall to wall carpeting, and a tall metal statue standing guard with a sword in his hand, dressed in armor. She wondered if he had in mind to be her knight in shining armor. She thought, maybe this is what she needed—someone to rescue her.

While Mercy and John were eating, he talked about his love for music. His favorites were opera classics, and the music from "The Man de la Mancha."[14] This gave her the opportunity to ask about the statue in the living room. He responded by telling her the story about Don Quixote and his love for Dulcinea del Toboso.[15] When he got up from the table and dramatically pranced around the room, flinging his arms as if he was engaged in a sword fight, she began to wonder if he imagined himself to be the knight Don Quixote, and perhaps he was hoping that she would be his Dulcinea.

Mercy and John spent the remainder of the evening sitting in the dimly lit living room on the sofa drinking coffee and listening to the music from "The Man de la Mancha," with him singing "The Impossible Dream." She complimented him on his deep baritone voice, and suggested that he could have been a professional singer. With a show of modesty, he accepted her compliment, and then proudly told her how he chose to go to school to become an electrical engineer instead. Then he went on to talk about how he spent time in the navy traveling to see most of the world, and how much he enjoyed the work he was doing now.

To Mercy's surprise, after listening to the music, John took her home. She certainly did not expect the evening to end this way. She had thought the dim lights and music was his way of getting her in a romantic

---

14   Music by Mitch Leigh, Lyrics by Joe Darion

15   Written Dale Wasserman, 1959

mood to go with him upstairs to the bedroom. To say the least, she was definitely impressed by the way he treated her with so much respect. But most of all, she now saw this man had money. She made up her mind—this is it—the man of her dreams and she was not about to let him go.

After that night, as Mercy began to know John better, her feelings for him began to change. He was not the kind of man she thought him to be when they first met; now she saw him as an educated, charming gentleman who knew how to treat a lady. In all their times together, he never before gave her any indication that he had a professional job, was a homeowner and was financially well off. In no way was John like Dan who spent every dime he made buying clothes and playing the last of the big time spenders.

The following week John picked Mercy up and took her to meetings as usual. Then on Saturday afternoon he called to say that he was coming to get her, and suggested that she pack an overnight bag to spend the night with him; in this way he could save time by not having to pick her up to take her to Mt Zion on Sunday morning. Without hesitation she agreed, and lit up like a Christmas tree as she was thinking how their relationship was getting serious. On Saturday when John picked Mercy up and she got in the car and noticed some large bags and boxes in the back seat, she asked him if he had gone shopping that morning. He said that he did and had a big surprise for her. She couldn't wait to see what the surprise was. When they got inside the house, he seemed more excited than she was as he immediately opened the bags and boxes. She couldn't believe her eyes when saw the dresses, suits, shoes and coat that he had brought for her. She was even more amazed when she tried everything on and saw that everything was a perfect fit. Like a child, she was so excited, and jumped up and down while thanking him all at the same time. Acting like what he did was no big thing, he simply said that he had noticed that she needed some new clothes and guessed her size.

Everything was fine until John said that he noticed that she needed some new clothes. Then Mercy felt insulted and angry to think that he thought that her clothes were not good enough to go out with him, and he had to buy her new ones. In all the times that they went out, Mercy always felt that she was dressed for the occasion in her very best, and he never gave her any indication otherwise. But if he felt this way, she would have preferred that he had taken her shopping with him to buy clothes that were more her style. Looking closely at what he brought, she could see that they were more his taste than hers. However, she made up her mind that she would wear them in order to please him. Mercy had no doubt about it, she was falling for John hook, line and sinker, and pleasing him was all that mattered.

On Sunday when Mercy and John went to Mt. Zion for worship service, she was all aglow, and during the service she thanked and praised the Lord like she never did before. She felt sure that God had given her the love that she had for years so desperately sort. As the weeks went by, Mercy and John attended AA meetings less as he took her to places that she had never gone before. He brought orchestra seats for her to see, for the first time, Broadway plays and concerts. And when he took her to the Metropolitan Opera House, she felt like royalty when the usher led them upstairs and opened the door to front row box seats.

It wasn't long before Mercy realized that John was not only acting like her knight Don Quixote, but he was her Pygmalion as well. He often spoke about how he was going to help her gain confidence and feel more secure. But it was not hard for her to recognize that he had ulterior motives; that he was really trying to make her over to fit into the mold of his impression of a woman with class. Nevertheless, she had fallen under his control and was letting him have his way with her. Just as Mercy was beginning to find herself; it was sad to see how she was allowing John to make her into someone else. Clearly she could see that everything that he did for her was for the purpose of teaching her what he considered to be the finer things in life: Broadway and the opera, how to dress, how to meditate, how to appreciate music. And in spite of his poor table manners, he also took her to some of the most luxurious restaurants in the city to introduce her to fine dining. However, no matter how sincere John's intentions were to help Mercy, he was giving her an inferior complex, and making her feel that she was not good enough for him.

One evening while Mercy and John were sitting in his living room, listening to romantic music sung by Johnny Mathis, he purposed that they should get married. But before she could respond, he said that he felt that he better tell her about his three previous marriages and divorces. Indeed, this unexpected revelation was a blow to her. She could not help but feel betrayed as she thought that they had been honest with each other and had kept no secrets regarding their past. During the course of their relationship she had revealed everything about herself, her previous marriage and divorce, her children and family. She even confessed how her drinking led her to do things that she was not proud of. Now she suspected that there were other secrets in his closet. When she got over the initial shock, she asked him why did he hold things back and not tell her about these marriages. In all their times together, she was led to believe that he had never been married. His only response was to say that his previous marriages did not last long—they just didn't work out—and he did not feel it was worth telling her about them. He also told her that there were no children involved, and denied having any kind of relationship with any of the women after their divorce. He then promised her that this time things were going to be different because he knew, without a doubt, their love was true.

Feeling a bit uneasy, she accepted his proposal

with reservations, not sure if getting married was the right thing for her to do at this time. Then, to her surprise, he got down on one knee, took her left hand and placed a diamond engagement ring on her finger. In that moment, she was so overwhelmed with mixed emotions that she burst out crying not knowing whether she was shedding tears of love, joy or sadness. However, all her feelings of mixed emotions and reservation were suddenly erased as he took her into his arms, dried her tears, and kissed all her fears away. Indeed, she had never known love like this before.

Except for Mercy purchasing her wedding dress and choosing her maid of honor, John made all the wedding plans. He decided on the date for their wedding, that it would be held at Mt. Zion with Rev. Moore officiating, and a small catered reception with only close family members and close friends. He also selected the place where the reception would be held, the menu, cake, and flowers. And without her knowledge, he even made reservations for their honeymoon on the Island of Barbados. He only included her in making the quests list. Again Mercy felt that he was holding something back when she saw none of John's family members, and only a few of his friends, on the guests list. It appeared as though it would be only her family members and friends attending their wedding. She could not help but notice how he became quite upset and annoyed when she asked him questions about his family. In an angry tone and disgust in his voice, he answered her by saying that his father was dead, his mother was in a hospital for the mentally ill, his sister and her family lived somewhere out west, and that he had no other close relatives. Mercy made a note to herself to never ask questions about John's family again.

The morning of her wedding, Mercy was awaken by the sounds of pots and pans rattling, the smell of bacon cooking on the stove, and the familiar voices of her children talking and laughing in the kitchen as they were preparing breakfast. Suddenly, the thought hit her hard like a ton of bricks: today she would be leaving the place that she had called home for most of her life. And she was overcome with grief at the thought of leaving the children that she gave birth to, and raised and loved and had grown so close to her heart. Her children were a part of her very being—they were her life, she lived for them. Although they were now adults and could take care of themselves, she had thought that she would never, ever leave them. As these thoughts were running though her mind and causing her so much pain, she broke down in tears and cried like a baby.

Instead of being the happiest day of Mercy's life, it was one of her saddest as she felt the same feelings that she had on her wedding day when she was sixteen years old. She began to realize that although she was now over forty years old in physical age, with only two years of sobriety, she was still spiritually and mentally a child. And on this wedding day, as it was twenty-five years ago, she was a child bride and too young to marry.

On the morning of her wedding, Mercy could no longer run from the truth and had to acknowledge how she had allowed the man she was about to marry to become her knight in shining armor who would save her. For sure, John had a savior complex and felt that Mercy needed to be saved; he was her Don Quixote and she was his Dolcenia. In addition, she was so insecure that she depended upon him to take control of her life, protect her and provide her with financial security. In this case he took advantage of her insecurity as he was a control freak. She could see how she had allowed the man she was about to marry to take the place of Jesus Christ as her savior, her protector, and provider. When Mercy finally became honest with herself, it was easy for her to recognize how closely she fit the textbook description of a dependent personality; she had replaced her dependency on alcohol to a dependency on a man.

There was no doubt in Mercy's mind that both she and John were very sick people spiritually and mentally, and were not ready for marriage. In no way could she say that this was a match made in heaven. Mercy had to admit to herself that she didn't really love John, that she was marrying him for all the wrong reasons. It was also hard for Mercy to believe that John really loved her. In any case, she felt that it was too late to turn back now. After all the plans he made and the money he spent for their wedding, she was too afraid to tell him she had changed her mind and was not going to marry him. Just as it was when she was sixteen, for the second time in her life she felt that she had to get married.

Therefore, even as her heart was not in it; Mercy got dressed and went to the church to get married as planned. It was comforting for her to see her mother, father, children, close relatives and friends seated in the sanctuary. And she was really surprised to see her AA sponsor and some AA members. Although she had invited them, she didn't expect that they would come. She could not help but notice how everyone was laughing and talking, and appearing to be happy to see her getting married. In her family, it seemed that the only thing that mattered was that he was a "good" Christian man, with a "good" job, a "nice" home, and was financially "well-off". Mercy made up her mind that if they were happy for her, she was going to be happy also and put on a "mask" of smiles to hide her face of sadness. As she walked down the aisle to the front of the sanctuary to meet her husband-to-be and saw that he was also full of smiles, Mercy wondered if John was also hiding behind a "mask." Indeed, the wedding ceremony seemed surreal, like it was not her, but an unknown woman with an unknown man standing before a minister repeating wedding vows. Mercy should have seen this as an omen of what their marriage was going to be like.

She kept her "mask" of smiles on at the reception and played the role of a happy bride. However, she might have fooled her family, but she certainly could not fool her sponsor or AA friends. They could see right through her; at one time or another all of them had worn the same "mask." Every time she looked their way, she felt like she was being exposed to everyone in the room. Mercy tried her best to avoid her AA friends and pretended that she was having a good time greeting the guest, and dancing with her new husband and family members. But there was no way she could avoid her sponsor who cornered her in the ladies room. Mercy became frighten by the way her sponsor spoke like a prophet saying that she could see John as a mad man, and he was going to cause her a lot of grief and pain. Upon hearing this Mercy felt shook up and angry at her sponsor for saying these things on her wedding day. Mercy didn't know what to say, but as she was walking out the door, she turned to face her sponsor and said, "Pray for me." Then she returned to her guest hiding behind the "mask" of smiles. Although she couldn't wait for the evening to end, she wasn't looking forward to going home with a man she hardly knew. And she couldn't help but wonder if she had sold her soul to the devil.

As John had planned, they spent their honeymoon at a cozy resort located on the tropical paradise island of Barbados. Mercy guessed that it must have cost him a fortune for their ocean view suite with sliding glass doors that opened to the patio and onto the beach. This was the kind of place that she had only seen in travel magazines. Everything seemed so unreal that she had to pinch herself to make sure that she was not dreaming. While John went into the room and sat down on the bed to rest after the long trip, like a child in fantasy land, Mercy threw open the doors to the patio and ran out onto the beach. She had never in her life seen anything more beautiful than the clear aqua blue ocean water that stretched out for miles, further than she could see, palm trees that were swayed by the ocean breeze, and the white sandy beach that looked so pure as if untouched by humans.

Everything was picture perfect. From the bed where he sitting, John could see Mercy and he was amused by her childlike behavior. Quickly, he got up and dressed in his swimming trucks and then went out on the beach to meet her. He suggested that she go inside to change into her bathing suit so that they could go swimming together. John did not appear to be at all surprised when Mercy told him that she could not swim. But he seemed pleased that this was something else he had to teach her. However, knowing how angry he can become, she knew better than to tell him about her fear of water and how she didn't want to get her hair wet. So she just started back to the room, saying that she was too tried to learn how to swim today, tomorrow would be a better day.

Like a scene in a movie, Mercy and John spent the first night of their honeymoon like two lovers holding hands, lying on the moon lit beach, gazing up at the bright stars displayed on a pitch black sky, while listening to the crescendo sounds of the ocean waves making music for their ears. It was so romantic. Feeling like an actress who did not know the script,

Mercy didn't say a word nor did she make a move. She was afraid that she would spoil the night by saying or doing something wrong. This was John's show and she was going to allow him to have his way. After all, he was in charge as the writer, producer, director, as well as the leading man. And he surely knew what he was doing. Later that night in the bedroom, all of her fears disappeared as he made love to her.

Mercy and John spent the week in Barbados on the beach and visiting the many tourist attractions. After the first day, he didn't say anything more about teaching her how to swim. He figured it out for himself that she was afraid of water and didn't want to get her hair wet. It would have been a fabulous honeymoon if her low self-esteem had only stayed out of the way. Every morning she stayed in the bathroom mirror for several hours putting on her makeup, combing her hair and putting on her cloths. He would often ask what was taking her so long to dress. She could never give him a satisfactory answer which annoyed him even more, especially since he told her not to wear any makeup, and to dress casual to go in the water or walk around in the hot sun. However, no matter what she had on, she never felt that she looked good enough for him. So all day long, whether on the beach or on tour, she went in and out of bathrooms to look in the mirror and to fix herself up.

CHAPTER 6

Married to Dr. Jekyll and Mr. Hyde

When their honeymoon was over, John returned to work and Mercy was left alone in the house with nothing to do but watch the television game shows, Soap Operas, and sitcoms. As with everything else, he was in charge of cleaning the house, shopping for groceries, and cooking the food (he did allow her to cook her own breakfast and lunch). Sometimes, with his instruction, he allowed her to help him do these things. But most of the time he did them by himself, treating her as if she was incapable of even doing housework. Feeling very uncomfortable and not at home, she usually sat in one spot on the sofa, afraid to move around or touch things. It was definitely "his house." And it seemed very mysterious and strange with all the rooms dark with wood paneling, and all the window covered with dark, heavy woven custom made shades that kept the light out. Some of the windows were even boarded up. Mercy would have loved to redecorate the house to make it look more feminine with brighter colors, curtains and drapes. However, she knew better to leave things as they were.

It wasn't long before the nightmare began. One evening John came home from work appearing disheveled with a strange look on his face, slurring his words and smelling like alcohol. Mercy was frightened to death since she heard that he could become extremely violent when he was drunk. She was told that this was one of the reasons why his previous wives divorced him. With him being such a large man and she being such a small woman, she could only image how much physical harm he could do to her. She decided that the best thing for her to do was to stay out of his way. As usual, he went into the kitchen and started to cook while she sat on the sofa in the living room pretending to watch the television.

After John finished cooking, he didn't eat, but stumbled upstairs and fell across the bed with his clothes on. He must have thought that he was preparing dinner for Mercy, but she wanted none of it. When she heard him snoring and knew that he was sound asleep, she felt it was safe to go into the kitchen. The mess was worse than she expected. There were onion peels, tomato sauce and spaghetti spilled all over the counter tops, stove and floor. All the cabinet doors were left wide open, and all the seasons and spices were on the table. The sink was full as if he used all the pots, pans and dishes that were in the house. The spaghetti, meat balls and tomato sauce that he left on the stove was half cooked and didn't look fit for anyone to eat, so she threw it all out. It took her hours to clean the stove, scrub all the pots and pans, wash all the dishes, and sweep and mop the floor. When Mercy finished, the kitchen never looked so good, it was sparkling clean while she was a mess after working so hard. She could do nothing more than to make a cheese sandwich to eat and a glass of juice, and then go to sleep in the spare bedroom. Indeed, Mercy was grateful that John never again attempted to cook dinner when he was drunk.

Mercy was surprised the next morning when she heard John up, taking a shower and getting dress to go to work, acting as if nothing had happened the night before. When he saw her in the spare bedroom, he wanted to know why she didn't sleep in the bed with him. When she told him how he came home from work drunk, and she thought it better not to disturb him, he apologized for coming home that way and told her not to make anything of it, it was only a slip. He blamed his slip on their not attending enough AA meetings, and promised that they would make meetings daily starting that evening when he came home from work. He also promised that he would be more active in church, continue to serve on the usher board and join her in teaching Sunday school.

However, John was not able to keep any of his promises as he kept coming home from work drunk. And as his drinking progressed, he started behaving like a wild man and turning his anger towards Mercy. Although he wasn't physically abusive, he was very intimidating and aggressive. She became a nervous wreck, trying to stay out of his way. Some days he came home so drunk and angry that she feared for her life, and had to run out of the house or hid under a table. Finally it came to the point when she could not take it any longer, him coming home drunk and behaving in this way. Therefore, she decided that she would leave him, and go back home to her children. Within a few days of her leaving, John came to get her, sober and acting like he couldn't understand why she left home; and he was innocent of any wrong doing. John might have thought that he was fooling her family; however Mercy could see how he was embarrassed and was trying to hide his shame behind a shield of pride. In spite of going against her better judgment, but feeling sorry for him, she went home with him anyway.

For about two weeks John stayed sober and Mercy was beginning to think that things at home were getting back to "normal." But that was not happening; he was really setting himself up for the next drink. He made meetings as unusual and never told his sponsor or anyone else about his slip. Like Mr. AA he went out on speaking engagements, telling others how to stay sober by going to meetings and practicing the Twelve

Steps. However, he was not doing any of these things. Much less he was not being honest with himself nor anyone else. In this way, it was not long before he was drunk. He followed a pattern of staying sober for a few weeks and sometimes even a month and then he would slip. Although she was afraid of John when he was drinking, she stayed with him and was able to keep her sanity and remain sober by attending meetings, and getting involved in AA as she was in the beginning of her sobriety. She also went to church every Sunday and left him at home when he was too drunk to go with her.

When John started drinking on the job, he was referred to the human resources department for counseling. The fear of losing his job kept him sober only for a short time; while in counseling he went to AA still in denial and going on speaking engagements as usual. And then, like before, he was soon drunk again. His drinking got so bad that he had to be hospitalized and admitted to the detoxification unit several times. One time after leaving the hospital, John maintained his sobriety for over a year and Mercy thought that at last he had stopped drinking. But this was not to be. The pattern continued for years, when he would stay sober for a while and then start drinking again. In the times when John was sober, they went on vacations in the Adirondack Mountains and cruises to the Caribbean Islands. And like old times, they went to see Broadway plays, concerts, and the Metropolitan Opera House. However, Mercy did not trust John.

So wherever they went she was always nervously watching to see if he was drinking.

Mercy thought that it was amazing how John got up early every morning and went to work no matter what condition he was in, and he never again took a drink on the job. It was also amazing how he was able to drive his car when he was drunk and not have a car accident or receive a DWI. However, things began to fall apart when he got to the point where he was no longer taking care of her, but she was taking care of him. Little by little, without his help she was going grocery shopping, cooking dinner, and cleaning the house. For him to lose control of things was really a blow to his pride and deflated his ego. The stress and tension in the house was thick enough to cut with a knife.

As time went by, Mercy recognized that John was becoming envious of her sobriety and became mentally abusive like he was trying to cause her to drink or drive her crazy. He criticized everything she did—nothing she did was ever right. Sometimes he would not eat the food she cooked. And when she didn't do what she was told, he would intimidate her by becoming angry and aggressive—almost explosive. She also was aware of how he was trying to make her jealous. When they went any place together—church, meetings, vacations—he would purposely flirt with other women in a way for her to see him. He even gave other women his telephone number to call the house and ask to speak to him.

When she brought these accusations to his attention, he acted as if he was innocent and said that it was all in her mind. For certain, it did not enter her mind that he could be involved with other women. That was the least of her concerns. In the physical shape that he was in, it was no way for him to have any kind of affair.

John was a changed man. He was no longer Mercy's knight in shining armor or her savior. Most of the time he behaved like a tyrant and his personality was like Dr. Jekyll and Mr. Hyde. She didn't know what to expect, and when he was drunk she could only expect the worse. And although he was not yet physically abusive, she feared for her life that the day would come soon. Just as her sponsor predicted on her wedding day, John became a mad man.

As her living situation was becoming unbearable, and Mercy was overwhelmed with fear, there were days when she was a nervous wreck, on edge and so depressed that she considered suicide as a way to escape. However, her religious belief prevented her from taking such a drastic step. Knowing that she needed help, she went to see her doctor who admitted her into the hospital to receive treatment for depression. She was in the hospital for a month. And during this time John stopped drinking and assumed his position of being in control. He also treated her like the doctor had proved him right, and he was justified in accusing her of not being of sound mind. But he was in for a big surprise if he was thinking that he had accomplished his mission to bring her down to build himself up.

During Mercy's stay in the hospital, with the help of the psychiatrist and group therapy sessions, she began to see things more clearly, and her eyes were opened to recognize how much she had depended upon her husband and not Jesus Christ as her Lord and Savior. And this was her downfall. After having such a profound spiritual awakening she saw John in a different light. He was only human and no longer would she allow him to take control of her life. Surely he was not capable of controlling her life while he couldn't even control his own life, much less control his drinking. Just like Don Quixote fighting the windmill, John was fighting with all of his might to take control over alcohol. But sadly his big ego got in the way of his seeing how he was fighting a losing battle. Clearly, both Mercy and John needed to turn their lives over to God and His Son Jesus Christ.

Mercy took advantage of the quiet time in the solitude of her hospital room to pray and meditate, and to draw closer to God; and through the therapeutic and the psychiatric care she received, she overcame her fears, gained confidence to believe in herself, and know that with God she was strong enough to handle whatever situations came her way. No doubt about it, this was the turning point in her life, and things for her would never be the same.

CHAPTER 7

Not His Will

Shortly after Mercy returned home from the hospital, she fell asleep while in the bed reading the newspaper. When she woke up, she noticed the newspaper lying before her turned to a page advertising schools. She didn't believe in coincidence and was sure that the Holy Spirit brought this page to her attention. For years, she had thought about returning to school to at least earn a high school diploma. In addition, in her childhood on Sundays when the family came home from church, she would preach to the stairs in the hallway. And all though her adult life she felt something from within calling her into the ministry. However, during those times women ministers were almost unheard of, and so she had a hard time accepting what she was feeling. But now having the faith to believe that all things were possible with God, she felt that she was ready to face the challenges to earn a high school diploma, an undergraduate degree, a graduate degree and whatever else it took to answer her call into the ministry.

When Mercy told John about her plans to return to school, he thought that it was a wonderful idea, and said that he would support her in anything that would improve her self-esteem and make her feel more secure. She dared not say anything about her plans to earn the degrees necessary for her to go into the ministry. She was convinced that if she told him this, he would not be supportive and would really treat her like she was crazy.

Once Mercy made the move to go back to school, she was truly amazed how God stepped in and all the doors were opened wide for her. She was most surprised to learn that some of the colleges where she inquired offered a program for students to earn a high school diploma in the freshman year. Immediately, she applied for admissions and was accepted at a college that offered this kind of program as well as a program where she could earn a Bachelor of Social Work degree. At registration for classes she was advised to write a Life Experience paper demonstrating her knowledge in the field to earn up to thirty-six college credits. After all the things that she went through in life, she was certain that she could write not only a paper, but a bestselling novel. And since she was unemployed with no income, she qualified for government financial grants that would pay her tuition in full.

It was hard for Mercy to believe that going back to school could be so easy. She wished that she had gone back years ago. But in those years she was too insecure to even attempt such a task. And it just wasn't her time. As she thought about it, she realized that God allowed her to go through the many years of suffering and pain in order to prepare her for His service. Now in helping others, she could be most effective in showing understanding and compassion as she could relate to their experiences. Without a doubt she could truly say, "I have had been there and done that." In addition she could be a witness of the great things that God can do, and give hope to the hopeless. Going to college was the best thing that ever happened to Mercy. She had never felt so good or been so happy in all of her life. Every day, wherever she went or whatever she did, there was always a song in her heart and a swing in her step. Indeed, Mercy felt "Free at last!" At last she had gained her independence, needing no one but Jesus.

The college was in another town; a two hour train ride from Mercy's home. She took advantage of the time reading, studying for exams and writing papers. In her first year she received the thirty-six credits for writing the Life Experience paper. She was an above average student passing all the exams with outstanding grades.

In Mercy's sophomore year the new pastor, Rev. Timothy Lighthouse at Mt. Zion Baptist Church, offered her a job as a director for a social service program that the Church was just starting. Although she was an exceptional student, she had no work experience in the field of social work and found it hard to believe that this position was offered to her, and she would also be paid a salary. She thought that she would have to graduate before getting any kind of employment. After discussing the offer with John, she accepted the position. He seemed to be just as excited as she was. He said that it would be good for her to have this work experience, and earn her own money. In addition, he said that he did not expect her to contribute any money towards the household; he would continue to pay the bills as he had been doing, and she could save her money and use it to buy what she needed for herself. Mercy was able to work out a schedule for her position at Mt Zion so that it would not interfere with her class room hours; and her position at the Church did not interfere in any way with her grades. Quite the contrary, the job helped her with school work as she was getting hands-on learning experience.

Mercy really felt independent when she received her first paycheck. It called for a celebration. That Saturday, she took the bus to downtown and went shopping. For the first time in her life, she able to buy the clothes she had only seen in magazines. She brought some things that she needed and some things that she wanted. When she finished shopping, she went home with bags and boxes filled with dresses, suits, hand bags and shoes. Although most of her paycheck was gone, she felt rich. Indeed, John was losing all control over her. However, to keep the peace, she continued to let him think that he was still in control. When she arrived home with her new clothes, she quickly modeled them for him, asking for his approval. With a bright smile on his face he said that she did a great job in picking clothing that were suitable for her, without spending a lot of money.

John could not help but notice how much she had changed. And like a proud sculptor, he treated Mercy like she was his work of art. He could not compliment her without reminding her that she would not have come this far without him, and with every compliment he added "If it wasn't for me." He was in his glory when he was helping her; he needed to be needed. So that she could have a place to study, write papers and homework, he turned the sun porch into an office, with a desk, typewriter, and file cabinet. When she had late classes, he would drive sixty miles each way to bring her home, so that she would not have to ride public transportation. As it was before he started drinking, he took over shopping, cooking and cleaning.

John was without a drink for more than a year. Their relationship was like the beginning; things were never better. He attended AA meeting daily, and when Mercy was not in school, they attended meetings together. Every Sunday they went to Mt. Zion Baptist Church, taught Sunday school and attended worship service. Once a month, he served as an usher. More than ever before they went to see

Broadway plays, concerts and the Metropolitan Opera House. Like a second honeymoon, they returned to Barbados. However, this time the trip was a whole lot different than it was the first time. Mercy was much more relaxed and could appreciate the clear aqua blue ocean and the white sandy beach. Although she still had not learned how to swim, she no longer feared the water, and so this time she even had the courage to go wading out into ocean. It didn't matter that her hair got soaking wet, and she could care less how it looked when it dried. She no longer took hours to dress in a pair of shorts and a tee shirt. John was very pleased to see her so relaxed.

As Mercy and John did on their honeymoon, they spent the first night in Barbados lying on the moon lit beach, gazing up at the stars shining against the pitch black sky, while listening to the crescendo sounds of the ocean. But unlike before, this time she could let go and be herself and not act according to his script. Feeling very romantic, she took the initiative to move closer to him. And then, like he was waiting for her to make such a move, he started kissing her with so much passion. They returned home acting like two lovers embracing and kissing like never before. He did whatever he could to make her happy, and she did the same for him. She was beginning to feel like he was her true love. It seemed like their marriage was going to last forever.

In Mercy's junior year, when it was time for her to do her internship, she was offered a full-time job with pay to work as a caseworker at a well-known human service agency. This was most unusual since interns generally worked part-time and only received a stipend. She was truly amazed how doors of opportunity were opening for her. But she had no doubt in her mind that it was God. She remembered Rev. Lighthouse assuring her, "Your God-given gift will make room for you."[16]

Mercy was able to change to evening classes in order to work during the day at the human service agency, and most Saturdays she would spend most of the day in the library. With such a busy schedule, she was not able to make meetings with John as she had in the past. And except for Sundays when they went to Mt Zion, she didn't spend much time with him. Although he didn't make any verbal complaints, she could see by the way he behaved that he didn't like the way she was managing her life without him. Knowing how he can become abusive when he was not in control, she knew that she had to go out of her way to make time for him. On Saturdays, when she didn't have to go to the library, she would suggest that they go out for dinner or to a movie. And whenever possible, she went with him on his AA speaking engagements. Often when she was writing a paper, she would ask for his opinion. And then she would be sorry for asking, since he was so opinionated, he would get angry when she didn't write the paper according to his point of view.

It seemed that Mercy was never tired. To the

---

16   Proverbs 18:16

contrary, she found strength and energy that she did not know she had. She loved going to school and her work at the human service agency. Her heart was in everything she did, and everything she did showed where her heart was. Even while she was working full-time, she continued to be an above average student throughout her junior year in college. And all of her job performance evaluations were excellent. In her senior year, she was placed in the excel program where she took graduate courses while in undergraduate school working towards her Bachelor degree. In this way, she would be a senior in her first year in graduate school, and would be eligible to earn a Master's degree in less than one year. As it was with all the others, she passed this program with outstanding grades, and graduated with honors.

On graduation day, John was beaming with pride in what he had accomplished. He took credit for giving Mercy the encouragement as well as confidence, and a sense of security that enabled her to go back to school. Indeed, he was in a festive mood. Like it was his graduation, he dressed for the occasion in his Sunday best. And after the graduation ceremony, he invited her family and friends to their home for a catered celebration. She had never seen him so happy. He played his favorite "Oldies" albums and everyone had a great time dancing and singing. Mercy couldn't remember when she had ever laughed and had so much fun with John.

That summer, she continued to work as a

caseworker at the human service agency. But since she was no longer in school, Mercy and John spent more time together. Very seldom were they seen apart from one another. They got up together in the morning, and after breakfast together, they would leave home together to go to work. He would drive her to the bus station, and then he would go on to his job. In the evening, after dinner they went to AA meetings together. On Saturdays, they spent time together going to shows. And on Sundays, they went to Mt. Zion together. It appeared as if they were making up for lost time. However, the truth was John was afraid that he might lose Mercy.

When it was time for their vacation, John took Mercy out west to visit his sister, Miriam, and her family. This was indeed a big surprise. Since that time when he became angry when she asked about his family, she was afraid to say anything about them. In all the years of their marriage, the both of them acted as if he had no family. She wondered why at this time he was taking her to meet his sister. What was he hiding all these years? At first Mercy thought perhaps John was staying away from his sister because he was ashamed of the way he had become such a drunken man. Now that he had been sober for several years and had cleared up, Miriam would never suspect how bad off he had become. But the more Mercy thought about it, the more she could understand how John felt that he had to wait to get her ready for Miriam's approval. Now that she had graduated from college and had a job, he could show her off. It was true, before she would have been very uncomfortable, felt out of place, and would not have known how to act around Miriam and her family. As Mercy was feeling very much at ease, they could enjoy their visit, and she would not embarrass John.

On their arrival, John and Miriam hugged each other so tightly that it was plain to see how much they loved one another. After so many years apart, Miriam and her family were so happy for him to visit them. John's sister even said that she feared that she would never see her brother again. Miriam and her family were not at all what Mercy expected. She was beautiful and a very intelligent woman, with a handsome, intelligent husband, and two lovely daughters. Mercy could see they were a "well-to-do family," living in an upper class neighborhood, in an expensive house with a swimming pool in the backyard. In no way could John have been ashamed of his sister and her family.

Miriam gave a party to introduce John and Mercy to her friends and neighbors. And Miriam went out of her way to make them feel welcome and at home. She was very friendly. In just a few hours Mercy and Miriam bonded, laughing and talking like they had known each other for years. John and Mercy spent a week with Miriam and her family, going sight-seeing, going to see a show, out for dinner, and to a dance. They were having so much fun that the time went by too quickly. When it was time to leave, everyone became very sad. Miriam tried to encourage them to look at some homes to buy and move out west where they could be together. John admitted that they would love to stay, but he and Mercy had to go back to their home and jobs.

These were the best of times, until Mercy started talking about registering for school to start the graduate program to earn a Master's degree. Then everything changed drastically. John insisted that she had no need to go any further in school. He tried to make her see his point of view: that she had enough education and a good job. What more could she want? Indeed, her education and her job had changed her way of thinking, and made her so sure of herself where she no longer felt that she had to always agree with him to keep the peace. She had her own opinions about things. Therefore she made up her mind that she was going to express herself and do whatever made her happy whether he liked it or not. So when she went against his will, and registered for school anyhow, the arguments began. After that, it seemed like all their conversations ended in disagreements. And whenever this happened, he would stop speaking to her—sometimes for days or even weeks. This did not matter much to her. Because when he was not speaking, she didn't feel as bad as before when her school work and her job didn't leave much time for them to spend together.

Unlike before, John didn't offer Mercy any support. He became very cruel. Dinner was no longer waiting for her when she arrived home from school. No matter how late at night her classes ended, he no longer came to drive her home. She had to ride public transportation and walk down the dark streets alone. Without a doubt, he was thinking that if things were bad enough, and she became too frightened to take public transportation and walk down the dark streets late at night, she would soon quit school. But she proved him to be wrong in his thinking. She was determined to get her Master's degree, and with God on her side, she feared absolutely nothing. Not even John. Therefore, she decided that she was going to learn how to drive and buy a car; in this way she would be able to drive herself to school, and back home late at night. However in no way was John going to allow this to happen, and made a plan to stop her.

One evening when Mercy came home from driving school, John said that he had to go to the supermarket, and asked her to drive his car. As soon as she turned the key in the car, he told her to forget what she had learned, because he was going to teach her to drive his way. From the moment she put the car in drive, he started correcting everything she did, and by the time they arrived in the supermarket parking lot she was a nervous wreck, and he was behaving like a mad man. That evening Mercy realized that if she continued to take driving lessons, this was going to create more problems in their marriage, so she decided that it would be best for her to give up taking driving lessons at this time.

After a while, John realized that while trying to persuade Mercy to do things his way, he was causing himself too much stress and also threatening his sobriety. He thought it best to leave her alone to do whatever she wanted, and he would go about his own way, doing whatever he wanted. Except for going to church on Sundays, they did only a few things together. He stopped taking her to see Broadway plays, concerts, the opera, or even out for dinner. And their last vacation together was spent with his sister and her family out west. It didn't take long for their marriage to begin to gradually fall apart. However, she was so caught up in her school work and her job she gave no attention to what was happening between the two of them.

As it was in undergraduate school, Mercy was an above average student with outstanding grades. The months seemed to fly by and it was not long before graduation day came again. This time John never gave her any kind of compliments or congratulations. To show his displeasure he acted like he didn't want to go to the ceremony, and dressed in a way to embarrass her. He wore an old brown suit that was too small with a tight fitting jacket and high-water pants, a red plaid shirt, a blue and green tie, and a pair of old shoes. Needless to say, he looked like a clown. And this time there was no graduation celebration at their home. He did even take her out to eat. He simply took her home and then he went out alone to an AA meeting.

Mercy was very hurt by the way John treated

her on graduation day. She could not believe that he went out and left her at home alone with no one to celebrate the occasion with. As she was starting to allow his behavior destroy her day and drive her into depression, she came to her senses and realized that his going out was the best thing that happened all day. She made up her mind to take advantage of this time to be alone with God; to thank Him for all the great thing He has done, and for all the great things He was about to do. And so instead of crying she began singing and shouting praises to God until she was caught up in the Spirit and felt His Presence in the room with her. Indeed, it was a great celebration like none she had ever experienced before. That evening when John came home, they had very little to say to each other. As Mercy was still feeling high on the Spirit, she preferred that he didn't speak and spoil her high.

The next day was Saturday, their day off from work. Mercy felt that this was a good time to tell John about her plans to go to seminary. This is when he really blew up. In no way could he tolerate the idea of her going to seminary. At first, he was too angry to speak, but just put his face down and held his head in both of his hands. And then, like a raging bull he started pounding his fist on the table as to release his anger. Seeing how mad he had become, she thought about how violent he was with his previous wives, and thanked God that he was not pounding his fist on her. After he gained composure of himself, he asked her to give him the reason why she felt the need to go to seminary. When she told him how she had received the calling from God to go into the ministry, he responded by saying she must be insane and hearing voices. He continued by saying that she didn't need another degree, after all, she had two already, and she had a good job, making a good salary with enough money to save as well throw away.

When Mercy went against John and registered for classes at the seminary, once again he became mentally abusive. As before, he criticized everything she did. But unlike before, this time his behavior towards her was more aggressive, explosive, and intimidating. In order to avoid John, after work in the evenings when she did not have classes, or on her days off from work, Mercy found peace and solace by going to St. Patrick's Cathedral. There, she would spend hours in the Lady Chapel on her knees talking to God. One evening, while she was deep in meditation, it was revealed to her how she had not completely turned her life over to Him. Then she had to confess before God, her wrongs and how much she had destroyed her life by giving all of her attention to finding a man, and making decisions regarding love and marriage without Him. After receiving this revelation and making her confession, Mercy vowed that henceforth God would be the number one man in her life, and she would give all of her attention to serving Him only. This meant that it would no longer be John's will, but God's will be done. And as his behavior became unbearable, she

made up her mind that she was not going to allow
him to drive her to the crazy house again or seriously
harm her. Mercy decided that it was time for her to
leave John.

CHAPTER 8

On Her Own

Knowing how explosive John can become, Mercy thought it was best to wait until she had found an apartment before telling him of her plans to move. So whenever she could get away without raising his suspicion, she went apartment hunting. As God was always with her leading the way, she soon found a beautiful, bright, sunny, affordable one bedroom co-op apartment in a well-kept gated community. When she learned that most of her neighbors were politicians, government employees, and professional people, she knew for sure that this was the place for her. Without hesitation, she filled out the application and left the required deposit. As she walked down the street, she couldn't help but sing and shout praises to God, paying no attention to the people looking at her as if she was crazy, out of her mind. Indeed, she was crazy for God. That evening when John came home from work, Mercy didn't say a word about the apartment thinking it would be better to talk to him on Sunday evening when they got home from worship service. Mercy thought that after singing the songs of Zion, praying and hearing the pastor's sermon, John would less likely become angry and violent.

Mercy found this to be true. After dinner on Sunday, while still sitting at the kitchen table, she started the conversation by talking about how their relationship had gone sour, how they were always arguing, and how stressful the situation had become between the two of them.

John said he was thinking the same way and was waiting for the right time to bring up the subject. And then before she could say anything about her leaving, in a calm and deliberate way as to put the blame on her, he said that it would be good for her to have some time to be away by herself, to get her mind together and then she could come back home.

Indeed, Mercy was taken aback as it sounded like John was asking her to leave, like she was to blame for the problems they were having in their marriage. This made her boiling mad; how dare him, she thought. In the past Mercy would have let John say whatever he wanted about her. However, now she was not going to let him get away with insinuating that there was something wrong with her mind. So boldly she stood up before him and said that if anything was wrong with her mind, he made her this way. After telling him how much she appreciated the way he helped her gain self-confidence and security, and encouraged her to go school, she expressed the way she felt sorry for him that he was unable to see the good in the fruit of his labor; how he should be proud to see the way she had grown to be secure and confident enough to speak her own mind. She pointed out how the problems in their marriage began when she gained the confidence to express her own opinions and stopped agreeing with him, this was the cause for most of their arguments.

Then defiantly, Mercy put her hands on her hips and stood face to face with John, and said that if anyone was to blame for anything he must know that he created the monster that she had become. And then she added that she was planning to leave before he suggested that she go away to get her mind together. Truly, John was amazed by the way she spoke up to him, and could see how much Mercy had changed. She was definitely not the same woman he married nine years ago. He assured her that he was not asking her to leave permanently. She responded by saying that she thought that it would best for both of them if she did.

Surely Mercy had shown John that she was no longer docile, but still he had a hard time letting go of his control of her. So when she told him about the co-op apartment that she had found, he offered to take out the mortgage and purchase the apartment in his name. And if that wasn't enough, he offered to go with her shopping for furniture, and after she selected what she wanted, he would pay for everything. Knowing how much he liked to be in control of things, none of his offers surprised her. As a matter of fact, she saw it to her benefit to let him have his way. With his excellent credit rating, he received approval for the mortgage without any problems, and his application for the apartment was unanimously accepted by the co-op board.

After the day Mercy told John that she was leaving him, they spent very little time together. It seemed like they were purposefully trying to avoid each other. She slept in the spare bedroom while he continued to sleep in the master bedroom. He even stopped going to Mt. Zion Baptist Church, after being an active member for many years. Mercy suspected the reason John stopped going to Church was because he was angry at Rev. Hightower for encouraging her to attend seminary, and go into the ministry. Whatever his reason, she made up her mind that in no way could he stop her from going to Church in the same way she did before she met him. So she took a cab to Church every Sunday and continued to teach Sunday school and participate in other church activities. And since she was at work during the day time hours, and attending classes at the seminary in the evening, she very seldom saw him. As she found the classes at the seminary to be more challenging than undergrad or graduate school, she spent most of her free time in the library studying for exams or writing a paper. Rarely did she come home for dinner but ate a light snack before class. Trying to keep up with her seminary assignments didn't allow her much time to attend AA meetings. Therefore, she didn't attend meetings that often, and she never went with him.

When Mercy and John went furniture shopping, she tried to show him consideration by selecting only a few low price pieces to meet her immediate needs, like a bed, a chair, and a table. However, he would not let her get away with this and insisted that he was going to completely furnish her apartment. Indeed, this was an offering she couldn't refuse. Like a child in a toy factory, she went about the store selecting sofa, love seat, chair, tables, and lamps for the living room; queen size bed and mattress, end tables, dresser, chest of draws and lamps for the bedroom; table and chairs for the dining room; and a table for the kitchen. As if that was not enough, he took her to a store to purchase custom made drapes and curtains, and then to another store to purchase pictures, and a crystal chandelier to hang over the dining room table. He wanted to make sure that she had everything she needed for her apartment, so they spent the entire day shopping. In all of her life, she had never gone shopping in this way. Although she went home exhausted, she found it hard to fall asleep that night, for she was so excited to have her own apartment to decorate according to her desire at any cost. When John saw Mercy so excited, he smiled with satisfaction feeling that it was worth every dollar he spent to make her happy.

In the last month before Mercy moved, she did

everything she could to express her appreciations for all John had done for her. She cleaned the entire house including shampooing the carpets, and polishing the furniture. She washed all the dirty cloths including the towels, and linens, and she ironed all of his cloths. Then on the last weekend she cooked his favorite meal.

Mercy couldn't believe how fast the time went by. In the final week with John she began to feel very sad and wondered if she was doing the right thing. After all, their marriage was not all bad. In the nine years they were together, there were some good times along with the bad ones. And she couldn't say that he was a bad man, but she believed he had some mental issues that he needed to deal with. And she had to admit that he had some very good qualities about him. He taught her a lot and took her to places she had never been. Uncontrollable tears came streaming down her face when she recalled the vacations and the good times they had together, For certain, she was never going to forget John and their marriage. Although she did not love him when they first got married, in the years that they had together, she had grown emotionally attached to him. Now as she was leaving, she realized how much he was a part of her, and felt that she was making a big mistake. But when she remembered his violent temper, and how she feared for her life, she knew that she was doing the right thing. None-the-less, parting was still very painful for her. Although John was good at hiding his emotions, Mercy could see how parting was just as painful for him. Over the years he had grown so accustom to having her around and was also emotionally attached to her.

On the morning of the closing for the purchase of the co-op apartment, John and Mercy traveled by the subway to the city, like strangers on the train they barely said a word to each other. While in the bank, reading and signing the papers, they spoke to each other in a courteous and polite manner, but everyone could easily see that there was tension between them. As the process took several hours, Mercy felt like she was going to become an emotional wreck and fall apart before it was over. However, John sat straight up, stiff as a board and spoke with authority trying to give the impression that he was in control. After the closing, she agreed to go to lunch with him, but was sorry she did when they sat in a booth across from one another with him going over the contracts and giving her instructions on how to pay the mortgage. To say the least, she had enough of him treating her as if she didn't know how read and couldn't wait to be rid of him.

On the day Mercy moved out, John left home early in the morning because he didn't want to breakdown in front of her. He thought that it was best for him to stay in AA meetings all day so that his sobriety would not be threatened. But when he came home that night, he didn't know what to do with himself. He had no appetite to eat, and he could not sleep. He felt so alone and the house felt so empty without her. The pain of losing her was so great that the thought of taking a drink to ease the pain came to his mind. But he knew better than to entertain such a thought. Therefore he went back out and stayed in AA meetings until he felt tired enough to fall asleep.

John missed Mercy so much that he found it very hard to stay away from her, so he went unannounced to visit her the first week she moved. When he showed up at her front door, she was so surprised to see him. He was not about to tell her how much he missed her. He just said that his reason for coming was to make sure she was alright and to see if she needed any help unpacking, arranging furniture, hanging pictures or hanging the chandelier. No question about it, she also missed him very much and was so happy to see him, and she surely needed his help to hang pictures and the chandelier. She wanted to run into his arms and hug and kiss him but she knew better. He would have to make the first move; and she knew this would never happen. No matter how much he wanted to hold her close in his arms, he wasn't about to show any sign of weakness. At all times he had to be in control, even of himself.

When John was finished working, Mercy invited him to stay for dinner. He went into the kitchen to look in the pots on the stove, and saw that she had cooked his favorite spaghetti and meat balls. He would have loved to stay for dinner but he didn't accept the invitation for fear he might get too comfortable. He was even afraid to sit down in a chair and rest for a moment; he felt that it was best to leave before things got out of hand. As she walked him to the door, he reached into his pocket and gave her five hundred dollars. He said that she could use the money to buy some dishes, pots, and pans, or whatever she needed. She gladly accepted the money, thanked him and kissed him on the cheek. He didn't return the kiss, but turned his back to her and walked out the door as he said goodbye.

The following week he came to visit carrying a large box in his hands. Like the first time, she didn't expect him. She was not only surprised to see him, but she was more surprised when he opened the box and she saw he had brought her a microwave oven. He said that he thought that she might need one to heat up her food since she was always on the run. She thanked him and invited him to sit awhile. Again, he declined the invitation saying that he didn't have time; he had to leave right away because he had an engagement to keep.

Mercy didn't see John again until they filed for the divorce a year later. Both of them were in agreement that he could file claiming that she abandoned him. Although he had said that she could come back home when she got her mind together, she had no intentions in going back. Life with John was like riding up and down on a cyclone, and Mercy was glad to get off. This was the first time in thirty-five years Mercy had lived alone and was not in a relationship with a man.

She enjoyed being single and wasn't about to give it up. As time heals all wounds, she no longer suffered from the pains of separation. After nine years of marriage it was over, they broke all ties, and he disappeared from her life. But John is the kind of man that's hard to forget. Through the years Mercy often thought about him and wondered if he was still sober.

When Mercy first left Dan there were times when she thought that she gave up too fast, that things might have been different if she stayed and worked things out with him. She believed what the Scriptures taught about divorce, and felt guilty until she spoke with Rev. Hightower who put her at ease by saying all marriages are not ordained by God. That she had to agree with. She remembered the days of her youth when she tried to give herself a man. That is how it was with her when she married Dan as well as John —she gave herself a man but God didn't have anything to do with it. Her first was a "shot gun" wedding, and then she had reservations when she got married the second time. As old folks say, she should have listened to her "right mind" and not her emotions.

Dan was a city slick womanizer and baby maker. And while Mercy was young and naïve he could easily take advantage of her. He was also a non-Christian man. She was raised to believe that the best men were found in church. So when she met John, a "Christian man," in the church she thought that she had a "good catch". Nevertheless, she found this not to be true. As she came to discover that there are as many devils in the church as there are in the street. She knew full well that just going to church does not make anyone a Christian.

After her divorce from John, Mercy was finished with men. From her past failed marriages, from what she saw the women in her family go through, and seeing how so many other women were abused and mistreated, she came to the conclusion that most men were no good and rotten to the core. In her life time she could not remember ever knowing a good and decent man who knew how to treat a woman. From her own personal experience, most of the men that she became involved with took advantage of her, all they wanted was sex, and after they were satisfied sexually, she never saw them again. She called these hit and run relationships. She met a lot of women that would agree with her—especially the women who never saw the man again after he "knocked her up." For this reason there are so many single mothers raising children without any support—financial or otherwise—from the baby's daddy. She called these men "dogs." At the battered women shelter where she worked she saw how some men used women as punching bags. This really turned her off. She had to admit that she might be wrong in her thinking that there were no good men to be found. But seeing how she and other women were so badly abused, she was too through with men.

CHAPTER 9

Her Friend in a Man's World

As Mercy was consumed with her job and theological studies, she no longer felt the need to have a man; she believed that she could do better by herself. Besides she did not have much time to even think about a man, much less could she afford to have a male relationship at this time. She literally slept with her books. Many nights she was up late writing papers or studying until three-o'-clock in the morning, and getting only three hours sleep before getting up to go to work. Her family wondered how she was able to do all of this, and expressed their concerns for her health. But she knew that she couldn't make it on her own. For certain, she had to pray a lot and depend upon God to equip her with strength and power to complete the tasks that was before her.

Since the clergy was clearly a male dominated field, Mercy was quite surprised to see the women outnumbered the men in her seminary classes. At Mt. Zion Baptist Church, as well as the different churches that she visited, all had male pastors and male ministers on staff. This could have caused her to wonder where she and the other women would fit in. Her mother even questioned why was she going to seminary. When she told her mother that she was studying to become an ordained minister, her mother corrected her and suggested that she study to become a Sunday school teacher since that was the role in the church for a woman. However, she could clearly see how this role was changing. With such a few men attending seminary, she was certain that there will come a time when there will be a shortage of men. At that time, she and the other women in her class will be ready to step into the pulpit.

Rev. Hightower recognized her calling and gave her his full support. He was unlike most members of the clergy. He was more of a trail blazer and supported women going into the ministry. While it still was unheard of, he was among the few pastors that licensed women to preach and ordained them. He also had women on his ministerial staff. These women sat on the pulpit and preached during Sunday worship services.

When it came time for her internship, Mercy was

certain that she could serve at Mt. Zion. However, when she spoke with Rev. Hightower, she was disappointed at his suggestion that she did this at another church. Since she had been at Mt. Zion from her youth, he felt that she needed a new experience. He promised to help her find a church that would accept her. Thus, he called Rev. Dr. Joshua King, Pastor at First Baptist Church, one of the country's historical churches with a very large congregation, and made an arrangement for her to have a meeting with him. When Mercy learned that Rev. Hightower had made such an arrangement, she became overwhelmed and felt like dropping out of seminary. But then she remembered the story in the Scriptures when God was sending Moses to speak to Pharaoh, and he complained that he was slow of speech and tongue.[17] Like Moses, she worried that she was not eloquent enough to speak at such a prestigious church where people from all around the world came to visit. Then she remembered God telling Moses, "I will be with you". In the same way God was with Moses, she believed that He would be with her wherever she went. She was also aware how her ego would get in the way, and she would be puffed up with pride if she was an eloquent speaker. For certain God could not use her if she was this way. Mercy knew without a doubt that God could only use her if she remained humble and depended on Him.

Therefore, Mercy spent a week praying and fasting in preparation for the meeting with Dr. King.

17   Exodus 3:10-21, 4:10-12

And, indeed, the Spirit of the Lord was upon her. Although Dr. King was a very popular man in the community and known around the world, Mercy was not a bit afraid to speak with him, and responded to his questions with confidence. In this way the interview went smoothly and she was successful in being accepted as an intern minister at First Baptist Church. She left Dr. King's office flying high on the Spirit. In all her wildest dreams, she had never imagined that she would ever serve at such a prestigious church. But now she was a witness to the Scripture that says that God "… is able to do immeasurably more than all that we ask or imagine, according to His power that works within us."[18]

As Mercy was leaving First Baptist she noticed two well groomed men dressed in suits and ties standing at the front door. One of them, a tall, distinguished man with mixed gray hair, walked up to her and said that he was a trustee at the Church and that his name was Joseph Hart. The other man who was shorter and appeared to be older followed him and said that he was also a trustee and that his name was Thomas Daniels. Then together, as if it was planned, they said that Dr. King appointed them to take care of all the female ministers. Of course she knew better since she had learned that First Baptist was among the churches that didn't have any women minister on staff. But she was flattered by the way they spoke to her like true gentlemen, and as she was not at all offended,

18   Ephesians 3:20

she stood quietly listening to them play their game. Then finally they admitted that they knew that she was coming to talk with Dr. King about doing her internship at First Baptist. After seeing her in his office, they decided to wait out front to welcome her to the Church. When Joseph noticed Mercy hailing a cab, he offered to drive her home, and she in no way felt threatened, accepted his offer.

As Joseph was driving Mercy home, he proudly talked about the organization that he founded and currently served as president. By the way he talked proudly about the members visiting the sick in the hospitals, raising money for the poor, and bringing the disabled to worship service on Sunday, she could see that he was a very caring man, and very different from the men that she had met in the past. She also thought that he was a good listener, as he paid close attention to her as she talked about her work at the homeless family shelter. But then she was most surprised when he told her that he was also a college graduate and had worked at a foster care agency before he retired. It seemed that they had a lot in common as they shared stories about their work in the human service field. Never before had she felt so relaxed riding in a car with a man and not having to put up her guard against his advances towards her. When he arrived at the door to her building, she thanked him for driving her home, they said good night, and she got out of the car without him asking for her telephone number or for a date. After years of suffering disrespect and abuse from the men of the world, she breathed a sigh of relief expecting that now as a minister in the church she had found a safe haven where the men of God would treat her with respect. But Mercy was in for a rude awakening as she came to recognize that these were hard times for women in the church. She soon found that some of the men of God were not much different than the men of the world.

On the first day of Mercy's internship at First Baptist, she was told that Dr. King and the ministerial staff were going out to attend the monthly meeting of the United Clergy Association. Although she knew that this was an all male Association that did not allow women membership, she asked Dr. King if she could go with him and the other ministers. He, being an advocator for equality and social justice, smiled and invited her to come along. Over the years Mercy had heard how this group of male clergy did not accept women ministers, and now she saw this as an opportunity to attend the meeting to see what they were all about. Mercy or Dr. King never said anything about her joining them. So she was caught by surprise when they arrived at the meeting and Dr. King walked up to the Association's membership secretary, Rev. Wright, and said that he had a candidate for membership. Rev. Wright then called for a meeting of the membership committee, and invited Dr. King and the ministers with him to come with them to the church study. As Mercy walked into the study with the other ministers, she was overcome with fear as she did not know what to expect, and she certainly had not planned to join the organization that day. At first, Rev. Wright and the committee members paid her no attention as they believed that she was Dr. King's secretary.

However, when Rev. Wright asked who the candidate for membership was and Dr. King pointed to Mercy, a tremendous uproar broke out in the room with all the men shouting at the same time, expressing opposition to women joining their organization. Ignoring her presence in the room, some of the members said some ugly things as they spoke out against women ministers. Some of the more conservative members tried to quiet things down by mentioning that their Constitution and By-laws stated that the United Clergy Association was an all male organization. And some of the members showed their ignorance by taking Scripture out of context, where Paul said that "women should remain silent in the churches[19]." Finally some of the younger progressive members suggested that it was time for a change in the Constitution and By-Laws. While the men shouted back and forth with each other, Mercy noticed that Dr. King and the ministers with him took no part in their unbecoming behavior, but just stood back and listened. And Mercy didn't say a word in her defense, but just sat quietly in a chair feeling rejected and in disbelief at the way the men felt so strongly against women ministers. Most of the older members made it

---

19   1 Corinthians 14:34-35

perfectly clear that for years the ministry was a man's world and they did not want to change.

The membership committee meeting ended with the members agreeing that it was time to change the Constitution and By-laws to include women. Before Mercy left the room Rev. Wright said that she should fill out the membership application and pay the fifty dollars annual dues, and she would be contacted when the Constitution was changed. Although she didn't want to be a part of any organization that didn't want her to be a part of them, she filled out the application and wrote the check so that the members would not think that they had frightened her away.

It took the United Clergy Association two years to change the Constitution. At that time her application for membership was accepted, and she was invited to join the Association. After taking the right-hand-of-fellowship for membership, Mercy did not attend any more meetings. However, as the first female member she broke through the barriers and opened the doors for other women to join the all male United Clergy Association, and some of the women have held leadership positions. Mercy realized that she was among the women pioneers treading on uncharted waters in a man's world. Indeed, this was an enormous challenge for a woman who held a negative view of men. However, as a servant for the Lord she knew that she had to let go of her pass.

Prior to Dr. King, none of the pastors at First Baptist allowed women to sit on the pulpit. And as much as he was a leading advocate for women in the ministry, he knew that he had to take it slow in bringing about changes since he was installed as Pastor less than two years ago. Therefore, when Mercy first came to the Church, Dr. King instructed her to sit in the congregation while all the male ministers sat on the pulpit and participated in the Sunday worship services. However, she did sit on the pulpit to preside over funeral services and Friday night prayer service. In addition, she taught Bible study classes, and provided leadership for some of the women groups. In this way most of the members at First Baptist got to know her and developed a relationship with her as well.

After she had been at the Church for several months, one Sunday Dr. King told Mercy to put on her robe and join the other ministers in the pulpit to participate in the worship service. When she walked up on the pulpit, to everyone's surprise, there was a loud thunder of applause from the congregation. Indeed, this was an historical moment as Mercy was the first woman to sit on the pulpit, and later preach, during the Sunday worship services at this world famous Church.

First Baptist had recently purchased a building to start a shelter for homeless families and needed someone to write the proposal, obtain funding, and direct the program. Although Mercy did not believe in co-incidences, she was still truly amazed to see how everything happened in divine order—how she was in the right place at the right time. Indeed, she came to First Baptist prepared by God to do the work that He had called her to do. She held a Bachelor's as well as a Master's degree in social work, and had work experience as a social worker in a shelter for homeless families. After reading her resume, Dr. King knew without a doubt that she was the one sent by God to develop the shelter, and he appointed her to be the Director of the Program. While the other student interns at First Baptist only received a stipend, she held a full-time position and was paid full-time wages. This she recognized as a blessing from God.

Although Dr. King advocated for equality and accepted women in the ministry, and Mercy was accepted by the members at First Baptist as well, still she felt out of place around the men and unsure about her role as a woman minister. In the man's world she felt all alone and was in desperate need of a role model and a woman's companionship. But the few women ministers she knew were not about to be a true friend as they saw her in the position they all desired. And most of these women were very envious of her and behaved like crabs in a barrel pulling each other down trying to the reach the top.

Joseph turned out to be the only true friend Mercy had. He was serious about his responsibility to take care of the female minister. After worship service, most Sundays Mercy and Joseph ate in First Baptist dining room, she with some of the members and he

COME, SEE A MAN

with friends, and then he would wait out front to drive her home. Whenever she had to work late in the evenings he would be in his car parked in front of the Church waiting to take her to get something to eat and take her home. And on the nights she had late classes, he would drive down town to the seminary to do the same. These occasions were never considered to be dates, but he wanted to make sure that she had at least one decent meal since these days started early in the morning into late at night, and she usually ate a lot of junk food. Most of the time, Joseph and Mercy went Dutch to inexpensive diners and fast food restaurants. Sometimes in a way to show her appreciation, she would pay the full check. Also taking into consideration that he was spending a lot of money on gas, picking her up and taking her home, at times she would offer to pay for gas, however he would not accept this offer.

Whenever Joseph drove Mercy home, he would pull the car up to the front door and let her out, say good night and drive away before she could invite him up to her apartment. Although he told her that he was recently separated from his wife, in the process of getting a divorce and lived alone, he never showed any desire to have a romantic relationship with her. The way that he behaved like a perfect gentlemen, made it very clear to her that they were just friends. She could have easily fallen for Joseph as he was good looking, tall dark and handsome, always well groomed, dressed in a suit and tie. For the first time with a man, she could relax, be herself, and enjoy being in his company. She could see he was lonely like her and needed someone to talk to. Whenever they were together, he talked a lot about the organization that he founded, the volunteer work that he was involved in, and the ministries that he belonged to at First Baptist. Without a doubt, Joseph was a devout Christian Man. With him, Mercy was not ashamed to talk about her past marriages, and her years of addiction to alcohol. She also talked about the ministries that she was active in prior to going to seminary, the jobs she held as a social worker, and her children.

CHAPTER 10
The Devil in Disguise

Like a lot of Christians, Mercy got too complacent and comfortable, forgetting to keep her guard up against temptation that is always out there in the world. She was soon to learn that the devil is always busy trying to hold on to his disciples, and ministers are not exempt. The further she got away from him and was drawing closer to God, becoming one of His disciples; the devil fiercely went after her weakest point. And he set his trap waiting for her to fall into it. Ignoring all the warning signs, Mercy fell.

Temptation came in the form of a man named Reuben. Mercy met him at a meeting held at First Baptist. As she came early and was sitting alone in the Church vestry thinking about the paper for school that she had to write that night, he came and sat down in the empty chair next to her. She was deep in thought and paid him little attention. However, he was very much aware of her and purposely took that seat. For several months he had watched her in the pulpit, was impressed by her preaching, and was determine to seize the opportunity to get to know her. Knowing that he interrupted her train of thought, Reuben apologized then asked if Mercy would mind if he sat next to her. Of course she accepted his apology and said that the chair was open for him. After introducing himself, he started a conversation by asking her about school and her work at First Baptist. While she was talking, the meeting was called to order and their conversation ended. However, now that he had her attention, he was not about to let her go.

When the meeting was over, before Mercy could get up from her chair, Reuben pulled out a pad and pencil, asking if he could get her telephone number so that he could call her and finish their conversation. Mercy had noticed him in the congregation during worship services on Sundays, and had also seen him around the Church during the week in various activities. Feeling that he was safe, she gave him her business card, and he did the same. Afraid that he would ask to take her home, she said good night and then hurried out to meet Joseph.

Joseph was at the meeting sitting with the other trustees. Not that it should have mattered, but Mercy couldn't help but wonder if he noticed her talking with Reuben. As usual, he was in the front of First Baptist, waiting to take her to get something to eat and take her home. So that he would not think that she had something to hide, she got into the car and immediately told him about her conversation with Reuben. Joseph admitted that he saw them talking, and then added that he knew Reuben well since he had been a member at First Baptist for many years, and they often had long conversations about the affairs of the Church. While they were eating and as he was driving her home, Mercy was surprise how much Joseph talked about Reuben. He felt that she should know that Reuben was a wealthy Wall Street Investment Broker who gave a lot of money to the Church. And as Joseph was driving up to Mercy's front door he asked if she planned to go out with Reuben. When she said that she would have to think about it, he responded by saying that Reuben was a nice enough guy, but he couldn't see how she would have time in her busy schedule to date anyone. From the tone of Joseph's voice, Mercy got the feeling that he was afraid of losing her friendship, and really didn't want her to see anyone other than himself.

When Mercy arrived home that evening, the paper that she had to write for school was the only thing that entered her mind, and she gave no further thought to going out with Reuben. Surely, she was caught off guard when he called two days later and invited her out for dinner on Saturday evening, and without hesitation she accepted his invitation. But then after hanging up the phone, she kicked herself for going against her better judgment, and remembered how she had promised herself that she would never again get involved in another romantic relationship. Since Joseph was her best friend, Mercy felt that she had to call to tell him that she had accepted Reuben's invitation to take her to dinner. Joseph simply said that he expected this would happen, and said that he hoped she would enjoy herself.

Unlike the past when she was trying to get a man, she didn't go crazy trying to figure out what to wear, but felt like her basic black suit and her dress black patent leather shoes were appropriate. On Saturday evening when he came to take her out, he rung the intercom and came up to her apartment, becoming the first man to visit her since her divorce from John. Unlike Joseph and the members at First Baptist, Reuben did not address her as Rev. Adams, but called her Mercy which she took as an indication that he was planning to have a familiar relationship with her. When he walked into her living room, she looked him up and down, and was not at all impressed. She saw how he was not at all handsome, and she would not have ever noticed him in a crowd. However, the expensive business suit and shoes that he was wearing made him look like money. And she almost fell off her feet when they went downstairs to his car, and he opened the door for her to get in the front seat of a Rolls Royce. Mercy had seen this car in front of the Church on Sunday mornings but never suspected that it belonged to Reuben.

As Reuben drove downtown, Mercy's old feelings

of insecurity and not being good enough came back, so she sat silently not knowing what to say. She breathed a sigh of relief when he broke the silence by saying that he wanted to finish the conversation they started the night of the Church meeting. After telling him that so much had happened since then, that she couldn't remember what they were talking about, he asked her to tell him what's been happening all week. She could see that he was not going to let her get away without saying anything; and so she nervously started talking, and didn't stop until he stopped the car in the front of a midtown Supper Club where the rich and famous hung out. As they were getting out of the car, an attendant came and took Reuben's keys to park it. Then he took her by the arm to walk down the red carpet under a brightly lit canopy, to be escorted into the building by the doorman.

From the moment Mercy and Reuben entered the Club they were greeted by the guests, and as they were led to a front row table by the host, Rueben stopped and shook hands with everyone they passed, and introduced her as Rev. Mercy Adams. Everyone she met greeted her with a bright smile and she did the same. She could tell that he was proud to be with her and she was proud to be with him. To be with such a well known wealthy man who knew so many important people, made her feel rich and famous as well. Mercy overcame her feelings of insecurity and not being good enough, and was determine to enjoy the evening.

Mercy was so happy to see the Club had live entertainment which meant that they would not be having too much conversation since they would be watching the show. When the waitress gave Mercy and Reuben the menu, he asked her if she saw anything on it that she would like to eat, if not, he would order the specialty of the house for both of them. Everything on the menu seemed foreign and expensive, so she said that he should order. Then he looked at the wine list and asked her if there was anything particular that she would like to drink. At first he looked at her with surprise when she said that she did not drink, and then he said that he understood that a lot of ministers were non-drinkers. Reuben had one glass of wine with his dinner and didn't drink anymore since he didn't believe in drinking and driving. While they dined on exquisite French cuisine, chorus girls danced, jazz musicians played, and a comedian told some clean and some not so clean jokes. She really enjoyed herself and couldn't remember when she laughed so much. Since she had been studying for exams and writing papers for school, in addition to working hard at First Baptist to develop the homeless program, she didn't have any kind of social life, and felt that it was good to be out.

Mercy left the Supper Club feeling so good and excited about having a night out that she couldn't help but appear like someone who had too much to drink. As Reuben was driving her home, they laughed and talked about the entertainers and his friends she met at the Club. When they arrived at her apartment building, he parked the car and said that he didn't want her to ride the elevator alone at that time of night. Not knowing him that well, she felt uneasy and suspicious of his intentions. When they arrived at her apartment, she unlocked the front door, then turned to thank him for a lovely evening, and then said good night. From the look on his face, she could tell that he expected to be invited in; but that was not going to happen. She had too many bad experiences with men taking advantage of her. Still, she didn't want to hurt his feelings, so she gave the excuse that it was late and she had to go to bed in order to be at the Church in time for the Sunday morning worship service. He smiled, gave her a kiss on the cheek, said goodnight, and that he looked forward to seeing her at Church.

Mercy saw Reuben sitting in his usual seat during the worship service and expected that he would stop by her office before leaving the Church. She was most surprised when he didn't, and hoped that he wasn't too upset when she didn't invite him in to her apartment the night before. A little disappointed, Mercy went to the dining room to have dinner, and as usual Joseph was there with his friends. After she ate and was on her way out the door of the building, Joseph met her with a funny look on his face, and asked if she was going home. Her bright smile was the answer to his question; he knew that she was happy to see him, and that made him happy. So he grabbed her by the arm and led her down the street to his car. As they were walking, Mercy could not help but wonder if Reuben was sitting in his car watching them. However, she could care less since he did not mean that much to her, and Joseph was her best and truest friend.

As soon as Mercy got into Joseph's car, he wanted to know how she enjoyed her date with Reuben. The way he asked the question, she suspected that he was kind of jealous of the attention she was giving Reuben. So as not to sound like she had too much fun, she told him about the Supper Club, the entertainment and Reuben's friends that she met. Joseph then warned her not to get too involved with Reuben because he would only hurt her the way he had done other women at First Baptist that became involved with him. When Joseph gave Mercy this warning, she immediately thought about her womanizing ex-husband Dan, and wanted to hear more about the women and what happened to their relationship with Reuben. Although he said that he didn't know too much about these relationships, she could tell that he was anxious to tell her about Reuben's reputation. While he was driving her home, Mercy paid close attention to what Joseph was saying and took his warning seriously.

Mercy didn't hear from Reuben until the middle of the week when he called to invite her to a reception for an African dignitary at the Mayor's Mansion on Saturday evening. Mercy accepted the invitation ignoring Joseph's warning, and reasoned that she had never gone to any affairs with African dignitaries; she didn't want to miss this opportunity and felt that it would not be any harm for her to go to such an affair with Reuben. Now knowing how Joseph felt about Reuben, Mercy thought that it was best not to tell him about her date.

Although Mercy had no intensions of becoming involved romantically, she wanted Reuben to continue to invite her to social affairs where she could make contact with some very important and influential people who could help her career in the ministry. This was certainly true of the reception at the Mayor's Mansion. Who's Who in politics, foreign dignitaries and members of the clergy were there. Again, Reuben was very proud to introduce her as Rev. Mercy Adams, one of the ministers at the world famous First Baptist, Director of the Church's Homeless Program, and a very dear friend of his. After his introduction, she only had to stand in one spot while the politicians, foreign dignitaries and members of the clergy flocked to her to ask questions about her ministry and exchange business cards. When the evening was over, Reuben drove her home, but this time he rode the elevator with her, stood in the hall to say good night, watched as she entered her apartment and then he left.

Like the Sunday before, Mercy saw Reuben seated in the congregation at the worship service, and then he left the Church without speaking to her. As usual, Joseph and Mercy ate in the Church dining room, and after eating, he was waiting out front to drive her home. When he asked what she did on Saturday, she gave him a half truth saying that she studied most of the day, and nothing was said about Reuben.

Again, early in the week Reuben called Mercy to invite her to a fund raiser that he was having at his home for a friend who was running for a seat in the State Assembly. She accepted the invitation, and on the evening of the affair, he sent a friend to drive her to his home. When she arrived in his neighborhood, she was not at all surprised to see him living among the very wealthy. All the homes looked like mini mansions, surrounded by well manicured lawns and flower gardens; these were the homes of her dreams. She could easily see that every detail of the furnishings in Reuben's home, from the crystal chandeliers to the plush carpets, were lavishly done by interior decorators and kept spotlessly clean by a housekeeper.

Reuben greeted her at the door and then took her around to meet the candidate and the other invited guests. Most of the people in the room were the ones that she met at the Supper Club. There were also some people from the entertainment field, and a few First Baptist members. After the candidate spoke, a small jazz combo played music while the guests mingled, ate hot hors d'oeuvres, sipped cocktails, and talked politics all evening. It was a very successful event with Reuben raising over five hundred thousand dollars for his friend's campaign. As the time was getting late, and she didn't want to hear anymore about politics, Reuben had his friend drive Mercy home.

The Sunday following Reuben's fund raiser, when he didn't attend worship service, Mercy suspected that his guests didn't leave until late that night, and he was too tired to get up the next morning to come to Church. When she arrived home on Sunday evening, she received a telephone call from Reuben. He spoke about how sorry he was to have missed worship service, and then after speaking about the affair at his home, he asked what her plans were for the next day which was a holiday. When she told him that she had nothing planned except to study, he asked if he could come to her place that afternoon to visit. Since she had been out with him several times and had been to his home, she felt that she could handle him, and said that it was okay for him to come.

On Monday afternoon Reuben arrived dressed casually in a jogging suit and sneakers, and carrying a bag of take-out fried chicken, potato salad, Cole slaw and donuts. It was plain for her to see that he was planning to spend the day. He had no problem making himself feel at home as he went into her kitchen to put the cold food in the refrigerator, and make a pot of coffee to have with the donuts. Thinking that a good movie would be a way to entertain him, she turned on the television to find one. However, when he came out of the kitchen, he asked her to turn the television off because he had some things that he wanted to say. Then he came and sat down next to her on the sofa and started telling her how he found her to be a very attractive, intelligent woman; how he was inspired by her sermons, and impressed by her theological views; that she was the kind of woman he was looking for.

From the moment he started talking, she knew where he was coming from since she had been around quite a few men who spoke similar words when they were trying to get next to her. But as he continued to talk, she felt that he was coming on too strong, especially when he said that he was falling in love with her and she was the woman that he planned to marry one day. Indeed, this was hard for her to believe, especially when he didn't propose nor did he say what day. When he had finished talking, he moved closer to her and asked how she felt about him. But before she could answer his question, he was posed to violate her.

Struck with fear and anger, Mercy told Reuben that she thought that it was best for him to leave. With an attitude, he stood up and apologized but didn't see how he did anything wrong, and then said he thought that she also had feelings for him. Trying to keep her cool, she responded by saying that she thought he was a nice gentleman and she liked going out with him; but she didn't know how he got the impression that their relationship was anything more. While he was standing in front of the mirror to comb his hair and straighten out his cloths, he said that he hoped that they could remain friends, and she would continue to go out with him. She said that would be okay as long as he didn't expect anything more.

A few days later, acting like nothing had changed Reuben called Mercy to invite her to a birthday party on Saturday. With reservations, she accepted the invitation. However, on Thursday she became ill with a very bad cold including fever and chills, and couldn't get out of bed to go to work or prepare a meal for herself. When she called Reuben to cancel their date and tell him how she was too sick to get out of bed and prepare a meal for herself, the only thing he said was that he was sorry she felt so bad and would not be able to go with him to the party on Saturday night. She was really hurt when he didn't ask if she needed anything or if he could bring her some food. If this was the kind of love he had for her, she felt that she could do better without him. Things were much different when she called Joseph to let him know that she was home sick and unable to go to the Church or to school. Without hesitation, he offered to bring her some food and some medication that would help heal her cold. There was no doubt in her mind that Joseph was her best friend and really cared about her. After that day, Mercy wanted nothing more to do with Reuben, and it was obvious that he felt the same way too. He stopped calling to invite her out on dates, and barely spoke when he saw her in Church.

The one lesson that Mercy learned from her relationship with Reuben, was the devil's favorite hang out was in the church because that is where he finds desperate lonely women who easily fall prey to his devilish schemes. She couldn't help but remember the story in the Bible that tells how Jesus was tempted by the devil that "showed him all the kingdoms of the world and their splendor, and said "All this I will give to you, if you bow down and worship me."[20] In the same way, Mercy felt that she was tempted by Reuben, a man of wealth who drove a Rolls Royce, introduced her to his rich and famous friends, knew the Who's Who, and lived in the home of her dreams. Certainly he expected that she would be impressed with all of this, and while she was hoping to gain some of his fortune, he could get all that he wanted from her. At one time she would have jumped at the opportunity. But now she was a changed woman. Mercy thanked God that she no longer desired material things to become one of the devil's disciples.

---

20   Matthew 4:1-11

Lover

How beautiful you are, my darling!
Oh, how beautiful!
Your eyes behind your veil are doves.
Your hair is like a flock of goats
descending from Mount Gilead.
Your teeth are like a flock of sheep just shorn,
coming up from the washing.
Each has its twin;
not one of them is alone.
Your lips are like a scarlet ribbon;
your mouth is lovely.
Your temples behind your veil
are like the halves of a pomegranate.
Your neck is like the tower of David,
but with elegance;
on it hang a thousand shields,
all of them shields of warriors.
Your two breasts are like two fawns,
like twin fawns of gazelle
that browse among the lilies.
Until the day breaks
and the shadows flee,
I will go to the mountain of myrrh
and to the hill of incense.
All beautiful you are my darling;
there is no flaw in you.[21]

---

21   Solomon's Song of Songs 4:1-7

CHAPTER 11

True Love

While Mercy was spending Saturdays, her only day off, getting ready to go out with Reuben in the evening, she was falling behind in her school assignments, doing her laundry, not seeing her family, and taking care of her other responsibilities. Now that she was rid of him, she had to use every free moment catching up with things. As she was starting the last year in seminary, she didn't have time for anyone except her children, parents, immediate family members, and Joseph. Indeed, he was happy to have her back to himself. Although after his warning she didn't tell him when she was going out with Reuben, he knew very well that she never stopped seeing him as there were no secrets at First Baptist.

Joseph made up his mind that he was not going to let Mercy get away from him again. He began calling her at home more often, and on Sundays after worship service he would invite her out to dinner. He stopped taking her to inexpensive diners and started taking her to expensive restaurants. Sometime after dinner he would take her to see a movie. And some Sundays after worship service at First Baptist, if another church was having a special program, they would have dinner there and attend the program. Whenever she had the time to shop and prepare food, she would invite him to her apartment for a home-cooked meal, and then they would just spend the evening watching television. Although they were spending a lot of time together in her apartment, unlike most of the men she ever dated, Joseph never tried to force himself on her. On all these occasions he was always a perfect gentleman and respected her celibacy.

On the Sunday after Joseph's divorce became final, he took Mercy out for dinner to celebrate the occasion. While they were eating, he asked her if they could be more than friends. This question certainly caught her off guard. So she looked at him with surprise and asked him what he meant. He then said that he had grown to have strong feelings for her which he believed was love, and he was hoping that she was feeling the same way. As she always wanted to be truthful to him, she took a moment to think before responding to his question. He continued to eat, while he attentively waited for her to say something. However, it seemed that she lost her appetite as she allowed her mind to take her back to Dan, the love of her life, and she had to admit what she called "love" was nothing more than a young girl's infatuation. And there was never any question in her mind if she was ever in love with John, but she was in love with his material possessions, the places he was introducing her to, and the positive things that he was doing for her. After searching her mind, she searched her heart and knew for sure that her feelings for Joseph were very much different from those she had before. Finally, in response to his question, Mercy said that she also believed that she loved Joseph in the way he has always shown his love for her. Like a dam that broke loose, water came gushing from Mercy's eyes as she cried tears of joy. She knew for sure this was it. There were no doubts in her mind that he was the man she longed for. From childhood Mercy searched for the true love that she had at last found with Joseph.

For the first time in Mercy's life, her best friend became her lover. Everything very much stayed the same as before. They continued to have dinner and spend time together on Sunday after worship service, and he also continued to pick her up at the Church after work, and at the seminary on the nights she had school. However, now he began to take her with him to social functions. He took her to birthday parties, anniversaries, and other celebrations to meet his family and friends, and he also invited her to go with him to several fund raising dinner dances. No matter where they went, he was never a stranger and everyone was happy to see him. He was so outgoing and so friendly—he spoke to every man and charmed all the ladies. He also loved to dance, and kept her on the floor most of the night. Like Fred Astaire and Ginger Rogers, they were such great partners. Mercy never before knew that she could have so much fun with Joseph and was sorry she had wasted her time with Reuben.

From the time Mercy met Joseph at First Baptist, her family heard about her friend and how he was taking care of her, and they was looking forward to meeting him. They finally got this opportunity when she invited him to Thanksgiving dinner at her parent's home. As usual, he was no stranger among her family and talked with them as if he had known them for years. And she was most surprised to see her mother laugh and hold him in conversation in a way she had never done before with any of her ex-husbands or friends. Everyone saw Joseph, not only to be a true Christian, but they also saw him to be a refined gentleman with perfect manners and class. After this first meeting, Joseph was accepted as a member of Mercy's family and they invited him to all of their holiday dinners, birthday parties, cook-outs, and other gatherings.

Early in the month of May when the birds were singing in the trees, the ducks were swimming in the pond, the air was pure and clean after the spring rains, and was filled with the fresh smell of flowers blooming with green grass spouting in the fields, love was blossoming everywhere; at this perfect time, Joseph proposed to Mercy. It happened on the Sunday following her graduation from seminary. After worship service, he drove out of town and into the country for her to see the beauty and wonders of nature, and to have dinner at a very exclusive restaurant. She thought to herself, nothing could have been more romantic. Then she was in awe as she walked into the restaurant and saw how luxurious and beautifully decorated the place was with vases of red roses, white linen cloths, expensive silverware and fine china on all the tables. And the wait service was the best—high class all the way.

From the exquisite menu they ordered for starters, Chilled Jumbo Shrimp & Mixed Green Salad; for the entree, Prime Rib of Beef, Baked Potato, Broccoli with Drawn Butter; for desert, Chocolate Cake and Coffee. But they barely touched any of their food as they were caught up in the intoxicating atmosphere of the softly candlelit room and the songs of love sung by Frank Sinatra. While Mercy was floating on cloud nine, Joseph proposed marriage and presented her with a diamond engagement ring. Without any hesitation she accepted the proposal and the ring.

After their engagement, Mercy and Joseph went together on vacation for a week at a resort in the country, but slept in separate beds, saving all acts of intimacy for their honeymoon. With him she learned that love was more than having sex. They had genuine fun just being in each other's company lounging by the pool, boating, dancing, sightseeing, laughing and talking. And while on vacation they made plans for their wedding. This time she had no reservations about getting married. There was no doubt in her mind that they were spiritually connected—a perfect match—made for each other; their marriage was predestined.

The Sunday before the wedding, Mercy was ordained by her pastor, Rev. Timothy Hightower, at Mt. Zion Baptist Church. It was a high holy day with family members and friends coming from near and far, along with Dr. Joshua King and the members of First Baptist Church. Members of the clergy, male and female, came from all over the city to lay hands on her. For sure, Mercy felt the Spirit of the Lord upon her. However, when she thought about the forgiveness of God to call a sinful woman to be His servant, she was overwhelmed with so many other feelings that were too hard for her describe.

The Friday following the ordination, Mercy and Joseph were married in a very romantic setting outdoors as the sun was going down, under a gazebo overlooking the Hudson River with family member and close friends in attendance. Mercy was all aglow dressed in a pink silk suit and carrying a bouquet of red roses. Looking very much like the distinguish gentleman he was, Joseph dressed in a black pin stripe suit, white shirt and black bow tie, stood at the altar waiting for his beautiful blushing bride. The reception was indeed a most joyous occasion with dinner and dancing held indoors at the restaurant. At the end of the evening, the happy couple was driven to the airport in a chauffeured limousine, then flew to Hawaii where they boarded a luxurious ship to go on a seven-day honeymoon cruise around the Island. Although this was not her first cruise, it was like none other before. This time she could really enjoy the sights of the ocean, and not anxiously keep a watchful eye on her husband to make sure that he did not drink. Each day the ship stopped at a different port for the passengers to go sightseeing. In all of her travels, Mercy had never seen a place more breathtakingly beautiful than the Island of Hawaii.

At one stop, they were invited to a Hawaii Luau. With the natives and passengers from the ship, they sat under the stars on the Hawaii shore eating roast pig, coconut pudding and poi. After their meal, they were entertained by Hawaiian girls twisting and swaying their grass skirted hips to the chants and soothing sounds of the guitar and ukulele. Mercy appeared to be in a trance as she stood on the side, twisting and swaying her hips along with the dancers, while Joseph watched his bride with love and admirations. Indeed, Mercy felt like she was lost in paradise, and enjoyed every moment of it. The fun was never ending. Every evening after dinner on the ship they were entertained by chorus girls, singers and comedians. Right after the shows, Mercy and Joseph went dancing to the music of Glenn Miller and other famous orchestras. Needless to say, they danced all night and never grew tired. When Mercy and Joseph finally went to bed, they were ready to cuddle up to enjoy the pleasure of true intimacy. This was the happiest time of her life—a real honeymoon. She was living a fairy tale, a dream come true. It was heavenly.

After two failed marriages and some bad relationships, at last Mercy met her match. Joseph was in no way as well-off as John nor was he as wealthy as Reuben. However, in retirement Joseph had a nice size savings, and along with social security, he was receiving a sizable pension, and with their combined income they had more money than they needed to provide for all of their needs and live comfortable. And after all that she had been through, she learned that it was better to be happy with a poor man than to be miserable with a rich one. As far as she was concerned, what really mattered was they had a lot in common and they shared a lot together. Most importantly, he was a man of faith and trust in God—a man who lived his faith. They worshipped together, prayed together, read the Scriptures daily, and tried their best to live according to the Word of God. Joseph was very proud to have an ordained minister for a wife and supported Mercy in everything she did. After her ordination, she returned to Mt Zion, her home church, to serve as an associate minister. Although Joseph had served as a distinguished trustee for many years at First Baptist, he gave that position up to be with her at Mt Zion.

In the first year of their marriage, Mercy and Joseph went house hunting. After several months of searching, they purchased a three bedroom town house in a new sub-division surrounded by trees and mountains, in the country. Being conservative, they furnished their new home with the furniture from her apartment, and purchased readymade curtains and drapes for the windows. Although their home was not lavishly decorated by interior decorators, their home was filled with peace and love, the things that money cannot buy. Mercy and Joseph found this to be true: "Home is where the heart is." In early spring, Mercy used her gardening skills to plant flowers and rose bushes while Joseph planted grass and mowed the lawn. In the summer, they invited their family members and friends to cookouts in their backyard. In the fall, they raked leaves and prepared their home for the winter. When the weather turned cold, and snow covered the ground, Mercy and Joseph snuggled up to each other by their wood burning fire place reminiscing the past and planning for the future.

Shortly after they settled down in their new home, Mercy was called to pastor Bethel (meaning House of God), and of course Joseph came with her and served as Assistant to the Pastor. Although he was not ordained, the title was unofficial and he was not on salary, the members recognized him this way and often referred to him as Rev. Hart. This is when Mercy realized that God matched her up with Joseph to send them into the harvest, as it is written, "He [Jesus] sent them out two by two."[22] Whenever the challenges became too much for her—whenever she felt overwhelmed—he

22   Mark 6:7

was always there to lift her up in prayer and give her the encouragement she needed in order to continue the work that God had called her to. In so many ways, Joseph was "the wind beneath her wings."

Most of the members at Bethel were very poor, and were only able to give a little money in the offering to support the Church. Therefore, they could only pay her a small salary, along with medical, retirement and death benefits, and no housing allowance. In order to pay their mortgage and bills, provide for their needs, and help support the Church, Joseph had to go out of retirement and go back to work. Members of Mt. Zion, First Baptist, and friends at other churches also supported Bethel, and gave beyond their tithes. In addition, the members had fund raising events that brought in quite a bit of money. In this way, Bethel was able to build a nice treasurer to keep the Church doors open and help those persons in need.

Along with serving the poor, Bethel was in the most violent, crime infested neighborhood in the city. Mercy was not at all surprised that God sent her to preach the Gospel to such people, as she could identify with all of them. Some of the members were destitute with only the clothes on their backs. While she was never destitute, she knew what it was like to be poor and on welfare. Some members were homeless, living in shelters and abandoned buildings. She knew what it was like to live in an abandoned building, although this was her home for only a short period. She had no fear of ex-cons since some of her best friends at one time were imprisoned for violent crimes, burglaries, murder, and rape. Although she never used crack, cocaine, or marijuana, but still the same, she once abused drugs with alcohol being her drug of choice. Besides her formal education, she had lived the life and experienced what most of the members were currently suffering. Indeed, she more than qualified to serve as Pastor for the congregation at Bethel. The members of the Church as well as her family and friends respected her as such, and no longer called her Mercy, but called her Rev. Adams-Hart.

When the members saw Mercy robed in the pulpit they could only see a saintly woman of God, and believed that she could never understand their pain and suffering. However when she preached the gospel, she often spoke about herself as a sinful woman who was changed by Jesus, letting the congregation know if He could change her, He could do the same for everyone—no matter how far down they had fallen or how great their sins might be. And whenever any member came to her seeking help or advice, she was quick to let them know that "she had been there and done that," and as they saw her in a different light, they spoke freely without fear that she would be judgmental. Mercy was like the woman who met Jesus at the well, and went out to the people saying, "Come, see a man who told me everything I have ever did. Could this be the Christ?"[23] Most of the people in the congregation believed her, and gained hope in Jesus.

---

23   John 4:29

In only a few months, the congregation doubled in size as Bethel became a safe haven that welcomed the people who were considered as outcasts. Some of those who joined the Church were elderly parents and grandparents, and had never been baptized or had never attended a church before. Soon after joining the Church many of them died, however, their family members rejoiced to know that their loved one had accepted Christ and had gone on to heaven. No one was ever turned away no matter how drugged up they were. Mercy could never forget the woman who came to Bethel high on drugs, with matted hair, needing a bath, and wearing only one shoe. Not paying any attention to the ushers or the congregation, in the middle of Mercy's sermon, the woman walked to the front of the Church to ask the Pastor if she could sing. Then Mercy stopped speaking and gave the woman immediate attention, recognizing her desperate cry for help. As high on drugs as she was, the woman stood up straight before the congregation and sung a hymn from the bottom of her soul. Everyone was touched, not only by her beautiful soprano voice, but by her feelings as well. After the worship service, one of the members of Bethel took the woman to her home to give her temporary shelter and cleaned her up. Indeed, the member of Bethel demonstrated her faith by helping someone who was in need. The following Sunday the woman came back to Church sober and looking like a different person. She accepted Christ, was baptized and became an active member at Bethel. With the help of Mercy, it wasn't long before the woman got a job, and was able to move into her own apartment. These stories are only two of the many examples how the doors of Bethel were always open to "Whoever will, let him come."

Using herself as an example, Mercy always encouraged the members at Bethel to improve themselves by getting a proper education or learning a trade in order to gain employment, and become self-sufficient as well as provide financial support for their families. A lot of the members at Bethel took her advice. One of the members felt that he was called to preach the gospel. Although he was a young man who was a recovering drug addict, and had never finished high school, Mercy did not want him to be discouraged. So she counseled him to earn his GED, and attend a Bible College. While he was attending school, Mercy trained him in the ministry, and once a month gave him a chance to preach a sermon during the worship service at Bethel. It was truly amazing to watch this young man grow in the Lord, and the members loved him. By the time he finished Bible College, he was ready to be licensed to preach. And it wasn't long after that when he was ready to be ordained and serve as Assistant Pastor at Bethel. Indeed, Mercy believed that everything works in divine order. When it was time for her to retire, the young man had enough training and experience to take over as Pastor at Bethel. As the members knew him and loved him as one of their own, he was unanimously accepted, and installed to serve as their Pastor. Just as the young man said, there was no doubt in Mercy's mind that the young man was called by God for a time such as this.

Immediately after the young man was called to serve as Pastor at Bethel, Mercy and Joseph retired and went to their home in the country to rest from their labor and enjoy each other's companionship. However, retirement for them did not mean doing nothing. They joined a church and became active in serving the Lord any way they could, as long as they were able. Indeed, Mercy and Joseph felt that they could never do enough to pay the Lord for all the goodness that he had done for them.

While in retirement, Mercy and Joseph enjoyed their life together traveling around the country by car, and going on vacations and cruises to places they had never been before. And as they grew old together, they were always there to care for one another in times of poor health and sicknesses, and to comfort one another in times of death and family problems. Needless to say, Mercy and Joseph lived happily ever after, in the same way that it is told in fairy tale story books.

Epilogue

Mercy could never forget how she came a long ways from her beginnings in the house on the forty acre farm in the south. At times her journey was hard with mountains to climb, valleys to go through, and rivers to cross. Still, she had no regrets, but only gave thanks and praises to God for the journey. For, by traveling the rough roads, she learned the true meaning of love.

Unfortunately, like Mercy, so many people try to fulfill their need for love without any understanding of the true meaning of the word. For love is the most misunderstood word in the English language. We use the same word to say we love God and also to say we love peanut butter, or a pair of shoes. However, in the Greek language there are several words to express love:

Agape is sacrificial love expecting nothing in return, as found in Jesus Christ who gave His life and died on the cross in order to redeem us from sin, "For God so loved the world that he gave his one and only Son, that whoever believes in him shall not perish but have eternal life."[24]

Agape is also human love, according to the apostle Paul, "Love is patient, love is kind, it does not envy, it does not boast, it is not proud. It is not rude, it is not self-seeking, it is not easily angered, it keeps no records of wrongs. Love does not delight in evil but rejoices with the truth. It always protects, always trusts, always hopes, always perseveres."[25]

Eros, intimacy, romantic and passionate love is the most popular understanding of love. However, love is more than a feeling; love involves the whole person, mind, body, and soul. When a person grows old and sexual feelings are gone, that person needs more than Viagra.

Phileo, brotherly love/love for others, the love of friends; this is the kind of love that is needed in relationships and is missing in many marriages.

---

24   John 3:16

25   1 Corinthians 13:4-7

Stergo, affection felt by parents for their children. The kind of love needed for children to grow up feeling self-worth, confident and emotionally secure.

As Mercy was raised in a family that did not display their love or affection, it must be said that her parents never intended to neglect their children in any way, but loved them, made sacrifices, and showed their love the best way they knew how, and raised their children in the same way they were raised. Thus, Mercy grew up with a misunderstanding of love; while a teenager her conception of love was the romantic love she read about between Rhett Butler and Scarlet O'Hara.[26] Therefore, as a young girl she started out searching for this kind of love in all the wrong places, with all the wrong men, and was almost destroyed in the process. Fortunately, Mercy grew up in a Christian household, studied the Bible, knew how to pray, and turned to God when her life was falling apart. Although her life got better after accepting Jesus Christ as her Lord and Savior, she had to suffer some more before she realized that she had devoted her life to searching for a man; while God was the Man she needed.

According to the Scriptures, we are taught that we have a jealous God,[27] and we are to have no other gods

---

26   Gone with the Wind by Margaret Mitchell, Macmillian Publishers, 1936

27   Exodus 20:5

(that includes a man) before Him. [28] The Scriptures also teaches us to "Love the Lord your God with all your heart, with all your soul and with all your strength."[29] Like Mercy, until we make God number one in our lives, and know the Love of God, we will always be searching and never finding true love. The readers should also know that there is no shame in seeking psychiatric or psychological help for their mental needs, in the same way they seek a doctor for their medical needs. Most of these men and women are gifted by God to help us in times of mental and physical illnesses, and He expects us to use these professionals.

God knows the women as well as the men who are emotionally scarred and suffer needlessly from mental depression as a result of their childhood or abusive relationships. Learn a lesson from Mercy: when she suffered from the disease of alcoholism, a psychiatrist admitted her to a detoxification unit where she received help to stop drinking. And when she suffered abuse from her husband, she had no problem going to a hospital where in prayer and meditation, she drew closer to God, overcame her fears and gained confidence to believe in herself with the help of a psychiatrist and a psycho-therapist. Indeed, while in the hospital she was made whole, spiritually, mentally and physically. For sure, this is God's will for us.

Like a lot of women, Mercy was married to a

28 Deuteronomy 5:7

29 Deuteronomy 6:5

man who was mentally abusive with her, but known to have been physically violent with other women. However, thank God that she left him before he caused her any bodily harm. Tragically, far too many women are involved in domestic violent relationships, and stay with the batterer until they are beaten half-to-death, murdered, or have the courage to leave. According to statistics, "On average more than three women are murdered by their husbands or boyfriends in the country every day."[30] I raised the question, "Why do women stay?" From my point of view, it appears that the women who find themselves in this type of relationship most often suffer from low self-esteem, feel badly about themselves, and are so desperate for a man, stay because they believe that they deserve the abuse that they receive, or think that they can't do any better. Indeed, these women must learn to love and accept themselves before they can expect someone else to love and accept them.

After reading this book, I pray that both women and men will come to recognize how much they need the love of God in their lives.

> *As the deer pants for streams of water, so my*
> *soul pants for you, O God.*
> *My soul thirsts for God, for the living God.*[31]

---

30   Bureau of Justice Statistics Crime Data Brief (2003), Intimate Partner Violence, 1993-2001

31   Psalm 42:1-2